DATE DUE

NB 2/68			
MAR 23 68			

RECORDS OF CIVILIZATION

SOURCES AND STUDIES

*Edited under the auspices of the
Department of History, Columbia University*

GENERAL EDITOR: W. T. H. Jackson, Professor of German and History

PAST EDITORS

1915-1926

James T. Shotwell, Bryce Professor Emeritus of the
History of International Relations

1926-1953

Austin P. Evans, Late Professor of History

1953-1962

Jacques Barzun, Seth Low Professor of History

Number XLI
Medieval Russian Laws

MEDIEVAL RUSSIAN LAWS

Translated by GEORGE VERNADSKY

1965
OCTAGON BOOKS, INC.
New York

342.47
M 468

Copyright 1947 Columbia University Press

*Reprinted 1965
by special arrangement with Columbia University Press*

OCTAGON BOOKS, INC.
175 FIFTH AVENUE
NEW YORK, N. Y. 10010

LIBRARY OF CONGRESS CATALOG CARD NUMBER: 65-25618

Printed in U.S.A. by
NOBLE OFFSET PRINTERS, INC.
NEW YORK 3, N. Y.

FOREWORD

THERE IS A CERTAIN timeliness in the publication of this little volume, comprising translations of the most important of the early Russian laws, in that it may make a modest contribution toward a correct understanding of present-day Russia and the Russians. Let no one dismiss this statement as fanciful; for the present has its roots deep in the past, and we need to learn something of that past in order properly to appreciate ideas and institutions of the present.

For this, translations are indispensable, not only of current books but also of basic works which illuminate the earlier history of the Russian people. And among these latter, it would be difficult to find more useful material than is here presented. These laws afford an insight into basic and relatively constant factors in the civilization of a people, the institutions by which they group themselves for social action, their concept of social controls, their sense of right and justice.

From the standpoint of the historian of social institutions there is interest also in a comparison between early Slavic law codes and those of other Europeans—the Anglo-Saxons, the Norwegians, and the Germans. As Doctor Vernadsky shows in his Introduction, there is much that is similar, and even some evidence of borrowing but there are also significant differences. The student of social and legal history will now have ready access to materials for such a comparative study.

The publication of this work has been facilitated by financial aid contributed by the Russian Translation Project of the American Council of Learned Societies and by Mr. Boris Pregel of New York City. It is a pleasure here to record appreciation of their generosity.

AUSTIN P. EVANS

Montrose, New York
1 December 1946

CONTENTS

INTRODUCTION 3

THE RUSSIAN LAW 26

The Short Version: Iaroslav's *Pravda*, 26; The *Pravda* of Iaroslav's Sons, 29

The Expanded Version: The Revised *Pravda* of Iaroslav's Sons, 35; Vladimir Monomach's Statute, 43; Other Enactments, 48

THE CHARTER OF DVINA LAND 57

THE CHARTER OF THE CITY OF PSKOV 61

THE CHARTER OF THE CITY OF NOVGOROD 83

GLOSSARY 93

BIBLIOGRAPHY 97

INDEX 101

MEDIEVAL RUSSIAN LAWS

INTRODUCTION

I

As was the case with other peoples, the Slavs had developed some general ideas on law and justice long before the appearance of written codes among them. The words *pravda* (law, justice, truth) and *zakon* (law, religion) are among the oldest words in the Slavic languages. Implicit in them are definite rules of social behavior that were observed by each East Slavic clan or tribe long before the establishment of princes of the Riurik dynasty in Kiev. With the promotion of princely legislation there developed a certain dualism in the East Slavic, or Russian, law. The social unit—tribe, community, guild—on one hand and the prince on the other are thus the two main factors in the development of Russian law and legislation. With Russia's conversion to Christianity (around 988), a third factor appeared—the church, which by that time already had for its guidance an elaborated system of canon law.

In that respect the evolution of the medieval Russian laws is similar to that of the Germanic laws. There is likewise a great similarity between the basic principles of the old Slavic common law and those of the Frankish and the Anglo-Saxon law. Many a parallel may be found in the Slavic and Frankish (or the Anglo-Saxon) court procedure, penal law, the role of the guild, and so on. It would be a mistake, however, to attribute the existence of all those parallels and similarities to the influence, at that early stage, of the Germanic law on the Slavic, or vice versa. The similarity must have been chiefly the result of the similarity in general conditions of life, in social organization, as well as in tribal mentality at a given stage of the historical progress of each of the two ethnic groups, rather than that of a conscious imitation on the part of either of them.

As the church struck its roots deep into Russian soil, as the authority of the Kievan prince extended over the whole of Russia (at that time, geographically, confined in the boundaries of what later became known as "European Russia"), in other words, as the Kievan state was stabilized, there arose a need for some coördination of the old tribal laws as well as for the compilation of legal manuals. Here again, the trends in Russian legal history are similar to the development of jurisprudence in Western Europe. As Pollock and Maitland put it, "our Germanic ancestors were no great penmen, and we know that the reduction of any part of their customary law to writing was in the first place due to foreign influence. Princes who had forsaken heathendom under the guidance of Roman clerks made haste, according to their lights, to imitate the ways of imperial and Christian Rome." [1] In like manner, the necessity of formulating in writing at least some of the Russian legal norms was first felt in the course of Russia's relations with the outside world. Thus, the two Russian-Byzantine treaties of the first half of the tenth century (911 and 945 respectively) may be considered, in part, the two earliest written documents of Russian law.

In the reign of Iaroslav the Wise (1015–1054), the first Russian code of laws was compiled. Known as *Pravda Russkaia*, The Russian Law, or Lex Russica, and Iaroslav's *Pravda*, this brief document is based upon the customary law and contains chiefly norms of penal law. There is a striking resemblance between some of its clauses and some of the provisions of King Alfred's Wessex laws.[2] Iaroslav's Lex Russica played in the development of Russian laws a role comparable to that of the Lex Salica in Frankish law.[3] Some twenty years after Iaroslav's death his sons brought about a number of additional ordinances tending chiefly to reinforce the princely authority. That collection is known as the *Pravda* of Iaroslav's sons. In it, considerable attention was paid to the better protection of princely servitors and estates, as a result of which the document, by its purpose,

---

[1] F. Pollock and F. W. Maitland, *The History of English Law*, 2d ed., I (Cambridge, 1911), 26.

[2] See W. Stubbs, *Select Charters*, 8th ed. (Oxford, 1905), p. 63. There is also some resemblance between the Russian laws and the Norwegian laws, but the latter were recorded in writing in the twelfth and thirteenth centuries only; see *The Earliest Norwegian Laws*, tr. from the Old Norwegian by Laurence M. Larson (New York, Columbia University Press, "Records of Civilization," 1935).

[3] On Lex Salica see H. Brunner, *Deutsche Rechtsgeschichte*, 2d ed., I (Leipzig, 1906), 427–442; A. Esmein, *Cours élémentaire d'histoire du droit français*, 14th ed. (Paris, 1921), pp. 93–98; Pollock and Maitland, *op. cit.*, I, 6, 13–14; R. Schröder, *Lehrbuch der deutschen Rechtsgeschichte*, 6th ed. (Berlin and Leipzig, 1922), pp. 257–264.

may be compared to some *Capitularia* of the Frankish kings, especially the *Capitulare de Villis*.⁴ Taken together, Iaroslav's *Pravda* and the *Pravda* of his sons are known as the Short Version of the *Pravda*. In the course of the twelfth century the whole code was considerably enlarged and revised. Thus, the so-called Expanded Version of the *Pravda* came into being; this served as an intermediary link between the rude and primitive code of Iaroslav and the much more elaborate "charters" of the city-republics of Pskov and Novgorod of the fourteenth and fifteenth centuries.

Lex Russica is not, however, the only monument of princely legislation in the pre-Mongolian period of Russian history. Separate charters, statutes, and ordinances were issued by princes on various occasions. Of these, only those issued for the benefit of the church, or of bishops and monasteries, have been preserved, in full or in part. Perhaps the most important among the documents of this kind is the Church Statute of Vladimir the Saint which may be called the cornerstone of church organization in medieval Russia. As will be shown later, certain groups of the population were subject to the ecclesiastical courts exclusively; therefore, statutes issued by church authorities should not be neglected in any general study of Russian legal history. It is noteworthy that one such statute, the so-called "Metropolitan's Justice" (*Pravosudie Mitropolichie*), but recently discovered,⁵ presents interesting parallels to some clauses of the *Pravda Russkaia*.

For the understanding of the general background of Russian jurisprudence in the Kievan period, intimate ties between the Russian and Byzantine law ⁶ should not be overlooked. Manuals of Byzantine law, especially the *Ecloga* of the eighth century and the *Prochiron* of the ninth, became known in Russia soon after her conversion to Christianity and eventually were translated into Slavic. A Bulgarian compilation of the Byzantine laws, known as the *Zakon*

---

⁴ On the *Capitulare de Villis* see Brunner, *op. cit.*, II (München and Leipzig, 1928), 97–98; A. Dopsch, *The Economic and Social Foundations of European Civilization* (New York, 1937), pp. 208, 328, 329.

⁵ S. V. Iushkov, "Pravosudie Mitropolichie," *Letopis zaniatii Arkheograficheskoi Komissii*, XXXV (1929), 115–120.

⁶ On Byzantine law see A. Albertoni, *Per una esposizione del diritto bizantino* (Imola, 1927); K. E. Zachariä von Lingenthal, *Geschichte des griechisch-römischen Rechts*, 3d ed. (Berlin, 1892).

Sudnyi Liudem ("Court Law for the People"),[7] the original version of which appeared not later than the tenth century, was extremely popular in Russia and, characteristically enough, in some collections of Russian law of the twelfth and early thirteenth centuries it was amalgamated with the *Pravda*. While no direct influence of the German law can be ascertained in the documents of the eleventh and early twelfth centuries, by the close of the twelfth century, the German expansion in the Baltic and, eventually, the organization of the Hanseatic League resulted in a lively commercial intercourse between the German Baltic and the north Russian cities. Commercial treaties concluded between the two groups in the course of the thirteenth and fourteenth centuries[8] played an important role in the development of some institutions of northwestern Russian law, as for example the judicial duel, which is first mentioned in the treaty of 1229 between the city of Smolensk and some of the German cities.

The role of those Russian-German treaties in Russian legal history may to a certain extent be likened to that of the Russian-Byzantine treaties of the tenth century. However, there was an important difference between the influence on Russian jurisprudence of the Byzantine law and that of the German. The Byzantine law—which was an historical extension of the Roman law—affected the very foundations of Russian juridical thought, creating the atmosphere in which Russian law developed in the Middle Ages. From the German law, on the contrary, only certain specific norms or institutions were borrowed in the laws of Novgorod and Pskov, the feudal spirit of the *Sachsenspiegel* (1220–1230) being entirely alien to Russian jurisprudence of the period.[9] Incidentally, even the German municipal law of the Middle Ages, the *Weichbild*, which, in the form of the so-called Magdeburg law,[10] extended to Poland, Lithuania, the Ukraine, and White Russia in the course of the thirteenth, fourteenth, and fifteenth centuries, is of much narrower scope than

---

[7] See T. Saturník, *Prispevky k sireni byzantskeho prava u Slovanu* (Prague, 1922), pp. 33–58.

[8] L. K. Goetz, *Deutsch-Russische Handelsverträge des Mittelalters* (Hamburg, 1916).

[9] On the *Sachsenspiegel* see Schröder, *op. cit.*, pp. 719–725; Eike von Repgow, *Der Sachsenspiegel*, tr. into modern German by H. C. Hirsch (Berlin and Leipzig, 1936).

[10] On Magdeburg law see Schröder, *op. cit.*, pp. 741–745.

the law of the northwestern Russian cities of the same period. While the Magdeburg law tended to assure immunity and special privileges to certain cities and to the merchant and artisan guilds within those cities, the north Russian law of the fourteenth and fifteenth centuries covered the status of the people at large.

The two outstanding juridical monuments of the period are the Charter of the City of Pskov (1397–1467) and the Charter of the City of Novgorod (1471); of the latter, unfortunately, we possess but a fragment. Another remarkable document of the same period is the Charter of Dvina Land, which was issued by the Grand Duke of Moscow in 1397. Here the ascendancy of Moscow is already felt, although the Charter itself represents a confirmation of the old usages rather than a declaration of the new monarchical principles. As the Moscow rulers extended their authority over more and more territories, charters similar to that of Dvina Land had to be issued from time to time in order to confirm the autonomy of a newly acquired province or to grant special privileges to the population of certain towns or village communes. Copies of a number of these charters, dated in the late fifteenth and early sixteenth centuries, have been preserved in local archives. The most important of them is the Beloozero Charter of 1488.

By the close of the fifteenth century most of central Russia was controlled by the Grand Duke of Moscow, and in 1497 a new Code of Laws effective in all of the territories subject to Moscow was issued. This Code was simultaneously a digest of the earlier laws and the first formulation of the basic principles of the new monarchical regime that was built upon both Mongol [11] and Byzantine foundations. Thus, the Code of 1497 brings to a close a fruitful period of Russian legal history and inaugurates a new and markedly different era— that of the Muscovite law.

Of all the various Russian codes, charters, and statutes issued prior to 1497 we have selected for translation in this volume the four most outstanding. They are the Russian Law (in both the Short and the Expanded Version), and the charters of the city of Pskov, of Novgorod, and of Dvina Land. Taken together they illuminate

---

[11] On Mongol law see V. A. Riasanovsky, *Customary Law of the Mongol Tribes* (Harbin, 1929), and *Fundamental Principles of Mongol Law* (Tientsin, 1937); G. Vernadsky, "The Scope and Contents of Chingis Khan's Yasa," *Harvard Journal of Asiatic Studies*, III (1938), 337–360.

the main trends in Russian legal history of the pre-Muscovite epoch. But more than that, they contain much material illustrating the general historical background of medieval Russia. No student of Russian history can afford to neglect the valuable evidence on old Russia's social and economic life that is to be found in many of these legal clauses. Thus, for example, the *Pravda* of Iaroslav's sons contains precious data on the administration of princely domains in the eleventh century as well as on the groups of population subject to the authority of the prince. The Statute of Vladimir Monomach—which is a part of the Expanded Version of the *Pravda*—uncovers the deep social gulf between the propertied classes and labor in Kievan Russia of the twelfth century. The charters of Pskov and Novgorod reflect the turbulent life of the north Russian democratic cities, their political strife, their powerful merchant class, their concern for securing fair protection to labor, and their basic concept of justice and equality for all before the law.

It is the attitude of both the Expanded Version of the *Pravda* and the north Russian city charters toward loans for interest which may be considered one of the most striking features of the medieval Russian law as compared with the Western law of the period. In the Roman Catholic countries of medieval Europe, under the influence of the church, any interest on loans was considered "usury." In Roman law, of course, "usury" (*usurae*) was simply the word for "interest" in the modern sense ("premium paid for the use of money," according to Webster). It goes without saying that the Greek Orthodox Church forbade the practice of "usury" in exactly the same words as did the Roman Catholic Church. Nevertheless, interest on loans was legalized both in the Byzantine [12] and the Russian jurisprudence. The failure of the Eastern Church in this matter, as contrasted with the partial success of the Western Church, is to be explained by the difference in economic background of the East and the West.

With all due reservations, one cannot but characterize the eco-

---

[12] It should be mentioned that of the Byzantine law manuals the *Ecloga* of the eighth century does not mention the matter, but both the *Prochiron* and the *Epanagoge* of the ninth century forbid taking any interest on loans; however, the *Basilica* of the tenth century reverts to Justinian's law, that is, to the recognition of interest on loans. See Zachariä von Lingenthal, *op. cit.*, pp. 308–312.

nomic regime of the early Middle Ages in the West as that of a "natural economy" based on agriculture.[13] On the other hand, "money economy" was one of the essential features of Byzantium.[14] As to Kievan Russia, its economic growth and blossoming was chiefly the result of an extensive commerce with both Byzantium and the Orient. A number of Russian historians now argue that agriculture must have been much more highly developed in Kievan Russia than had hitherto been supposed. Even granted that this was the case, the outstanding role of commerce in medieval Russia cannot be denied. Not only was there then in Russia a strong merchant class, but the princes themselves invested heavily in both overland and oversea commercial transactions. Loans at interest constituted an important corollary of such transactions. There was no alternative to legalizing them. This situation is duly reflected in the Russian law of the period.

II

While there is a great difference between the component parts of the Russian Law (*Pravda Russkaia*) of the eleventh and twelfth centuries, as well as between the Russian Law as a whole and the charters of Novgorod and Pskov, all these codes are based upon the same principles of court procedure. It would seem proper therefore to give here a brief outline of the characteristic features of the medieval Russian courts and court procedure.[15] Such an outline might also be helpful for a better understanding of the single clauses in each code.

As has been already mentioned, the people, the princes, and the church were the three main factors in the development of Russian legislation. The influence of these three factors may be felt—to a different degree in regard to each—both in the organization of the courts and in the court procedure. In the oldest part of the Russian Law—Iaroslav's *Pravda*—we find a coöperation between the courts

---

[13] H. Pirenne, *Economic and Social History of Medieval Europe* (New York, 1937), pp. 7–9, 12–13.

[14] L. Brentano, "Die byzantinische Volkswirtschaft," *Schmollers Jahrbuch für Gesetzgebung, Verwaltung und Volkswirtschaft*, XLI (1917), 569–614.

[15] The best general survey of the history of the Russian court procedure is V. F. Vladimirsky-Budanov, *Obzor istorii russkogo prava* (Petrograd and Kiev, 1915).

of the prince and the institutions of the people. In the *Pravda* of Iaroslav's sons, as well as in the Expanded Version of the *Pravda*, the princely court is obviously the dominant institution. By contrast, in the Novgorod and the Pskov charters we find a combination of the princely courts and the people's courts, together with the church courts. In Novgorod, there is a division of competence in judicial matters between the prince and the city authorities. The prince and his officials conduct most of the criminal cases. Of the city authorities, the mayor (*posadnik*) is in charge of litigation about land and the chiliarch (*tysiatsky*) is responsible chiefly for litigation concerning commercial transactions. Similarly in Pskov, the princely and city authorities coöperated in legal matters.

Everywhere in medieval Russia, all citizens were subject to the church courts in ecclesiastical matters, including marriage and divorce; church people—not only the clergy but every kind of attendant, as well as peasants and laborers on church estates—were subject to the bishop's court in all litigation. Cases involving laymen and churchmen were tried jointly by lay and church authorities. In court procedures, the optional steps permitted to both of the litigants played a very important role (see pp. 66, 67, 78–81). The role of the judge was limited to supervising the contest and equalizing the means and chances of the litigants. There were very few instances, if any, of participation by the state in a trial in the capacity of a claimant, or of any inquisitorial system of procedure.

Prior to the hearing of the case, the state authorities did not interfere in the negotiations between the contestants. Only after they had agreed among themselves about the subject matter of their litigation, as well as about the time of their appearance before the court, did they ask the judge to approve their agreement. The judge had then to issue a "term-writ," which was to be properly signed and sealed. Not until this had been done, could the matter be formally accepted by the court; thereafter there was no further opportunity for a free agreement between the litigants.[16] Prior to the issue of the term-writ the attitude of the state authorities was passive. The local community or guild was of greater assistance to a plaintiff who had difficulty in establishing the identity of the defendant. For example, a man who had lost something, or from whom something had been

---

[16] See the Novgorod Charter, Articles 30, 31, 34, 39 (pp. 89–91).

stolen, could make an announcement of his loss in the market place of his town. If the article was not surrendered within three days, anyone found holding it after the expiration of this period was considered the thief—that is, the defendant in the case. If, before the end of three days, the owner found his property in another man's possession or in another town, the possessor could reject the accusation of theft by stating that he had bought it from a third party, in a bona fide transaction. He was, however, to assist the owner in establishing the identity of the seller. This was done by means of the so-called *svod* ("confrontment"), an important feature of medieval Russian pre-court procedure.[17] This institution was similar to *Schub* in the Germanic law; [18] in Anglo-Saxon it was known as *team*.[19] It appears to have been much more highly developed in Russian law than in Germanic, however, and was more generally applied in Russia than in the countries of Romano-Germanic Europe.[20]

The modes of proof at the disposal of the contestants at the court trial were threefold: witnesses; appeal to God's judgment; and, in civil litigations, deeds, notes, and other documents.

1. According to the Russian Law, there were two kinds of witnesses: the eyewitness (*vidok*), and the witness proper (*poslukh*). Later texts deal with the second classification only. The role of the *poslukh* was much more important than that of a witness in modern procedure. He was an active factor throughout the proceedings. For example, according to the Pskov charter, in certain cases a *poslukh* was required to accompany one of the contestants in a duel.[21] According to the laws of Novgorod and Pskov, only one *poslukh* was recognized by the court in each lawsuit.

2. There were several means whereby people in the Middle Ages —not only in Russia—believed God's will could be revealed to them. The habitual approach to God in the court procedure was to have one of the contestants, or the witness, take the oath (in old Russian, *rotá*). In Novgorod and Pskov, the oath was accompanied by kissing the

---

[17] See the Expanded Version, Articles 34–39 (pp. 40–41).
[18] Brunner, *op. cit.*, II, 655, 659.
[19] Pollock and Maitland, *op. cit.*, I, 59.
[20] Characteristically enough, L. K. Goetz, the German translator of the *Pravda Russkaia*, did not recognize in the *svod* a Slavic counterpart of the Germanic *Schub*. Goetz translates the term *svod* as "Ermittelung."
[21] Pskov Charter, Sections 20, 21 (pp. 65, 66).

cross. Another method of appealing to God's judgment was through the ordeals—by water or by iron. The oath as well as the ordeals were known not only to the Russian but to the German law as well. Moreover, in some cases the German law also recommended the judicial duel (*Zweikampf*). This institution is not mentioned in the *Pravda Russkaia*. It constituted, however, an important feature of the Novgorod and Pskov laws and presumably was borrowed from the German law. A judicial duel did not necessarily end in the death of either contestant; when one of them was knocked to the ground, he was recognized as the loser.

3. Deeds and other documents were valid only when certified by public authorities. In Pskov, copies of all such documents had to be filed with the office of the archives at the Holy Trinity Cathedral.

A few words may be added concerning old Russian penal law. In the *Pravda Russkaia* the transition from blood revenge to punishment of the criminal by the state has been recorded. State punishment, in the period of the *Pravda*, consisted in the prince's imposing a "composition" (money fine) on the criminal. It is noteworthy that the *Pravda* does not impose any capital punishment, and recommends corporal punishment only once and in regard to slaves only. On the other hand, both in the Dvina charter and in the Novgorod and Pskov laws we find several clauses recommending capital punishment for certain crimes. As to corporal punishment, the Dvina charter recommends the branding of thieves, while the Pskov charter prescribes stocks for a rioter in the court hall (this was not so much a punishment, however, as a preventive measure). Presumably, the introduction of capital punishment into the Russian legislation was the result of the influence of the German law on one hand (in western Russia), and of the Mongol law on the other (in eastern Russia).

III

Let us now examine one by one the four legal monuments selected for publication in this volume, starting with the oldest—the *Pravda Russkaia*—which may be called the cornerstone of medieval Russian jurisprudence.[22] It was one of the sources of the Novgorod, Pskov,

---

[22] For the literature of the *Pravda Russkaia* see Bibliography at the end of this volume.

and Dvina charters as well as that of the Lithuanian Statute of the sixteenth century. As has been already mentioned, the *Pravda* is represented by two different versions, the Short and the Expanded. There is also a third, called the Abridged Version. This is allegedly an abridgment of the Expanded Version, although recently M. N. Tikhomirov has suggested that the original may have been compiled prior to the codification of the Expanded Version and may have served as one of the sources of the latter. We may disregard the Abridged Version here, since all of its clauses are found in the Expanded Version.

Eleven manuscript copies of the Short Version of the *Pravda* exist; three other copies were known to V. N. Tatishchev, a prominent Russian historian of the eighteenth century, but these have since been lost. Most of the known copies date from the eighteenth century, and it seems that most if not all of them reproduce the text of an identical earlier copy. Thus, for practical reasons, only two basic copies of the Short Version need be taken into consideration. Both were made in the fifteenth century, one now being known as the Academy copy and the other as the Archaeographic Commission copy. It is believed that the Academy copy best preserves the main features of the original.

Of the Expanded Version, more than ninety manuscript copies are known. They have been classified in several "groups" and "families." The earliest is the Synodal copy, dated 1282. It is, however, the so-called Trinity copy (*Troitsky spisok*) of the fourteenth century that must be considered closest to the original.

Most of the copies of the *Pravda* differ more or less in content, vocabulary, and spelling. Immense work was required to classify the main families of the manuscripts, to collate them, to assay the contents of their clauses, and to produce critical editions of the texts. V. N. Tatishchev may be called the pioneer in the study of the Russian Law. In 1738 he discovered one of the early manuscripts of the *Pravda* and started preparing it for publication. In 1749 he submitted it to the Academy of Sciences which, however, did not hasten to publish it—the work did not appear until 1786. Meanwhile, in 1767 a noted German scholar, A. L. Schloezer, who was at that time an associate of the Russian Academy of Sciences, published the text of the *Pravda* from a different manuscript copy. It would be out of place to enumerate here all the editions of the *Pravda* that were published in the course of the nineteenth century. Suffice it to refer the reader to the more recent editions. In Volume I of his *Das russische Recht* (1910), L. K. Goetz reproduced one of the best Russian editions then available—that of V. I. Sergeevich (originally published in 1904)—and supplied a German translation. In 1935 the Ukrainian Academy of Sciences published a new edition of the *Pravda* edited by S. V. Iushkov. It contained the texts of the main "families" of the two versions, with all variants. Full as Iushkov's edition was, it has now been superseded by the edition of the Historical Institute of the Academy of Sciences of the U.S.S.R. under the editorship of B. D. Grekov. This may be considered a definitive edition, unless, of course, other manuscripts are discovered in the future.

The Short Version consists of two parts: Iaroslav's *Pravda*, and the *Pravda* of Iaroslav's sons. It is known that, according to the chronicles, Iaroslav granted important charters to the city of Novgorod in 1016 and in 1019. After the death of Prince Vladimir (1015), there followed a protracted strife between his sons, in which Iaroslav finally overpowered his opponents and occupied the throne of Kiev. The loyalty of the Novgorodians to him was one of the important factors in his victory, and it is natural that they expected some reward in the form of certain political and civil guarantees. It is in answer to these claims that Iaroslav must have issued the charters mentioned in the chronicles. Whether any of those charters was identical with Iaroslav's *Pravda* is not known. In any case his *Pravda* must be connected with his Novgorod charters in one way or another. And, indeed, Section 1 of his *Pravda* guarantees equal consideration to Kievan Russians and to Novgorodian Slavs by making the man of each group worth the normal wergeld of 40 *grivna*.

However, the core of Iaroslav's *Pravda* must be much older than the beginning of the eleventh century. It is apparent that Iaroslav codified old customary laws, adding a few ordinances of his own. The Russian Customary Law (*Zakon Russkii*) is mentioned in the Russo-Byzantine treaty of 945. The customs themselves must have originated long before that time.

The *Pravda* of Iaroslav's sons was the fruit of the sons' legislation and was intended to supplement their father's code. The new laws were eventually codified and the new code was approved at a meeting of the three princes and their councilors, held, presumably, at

Vyshgorod in 1072.²³ It is obvious that the chief objective of the three brothers was to enforce the authority of the prince by prescribing the payment of a double "bloodwite" for the murder of their high officials and by protecting the servitors on their domains by a system of fines. The *Pravda* of Iaroslav's sons is thus not a general code of laws but rather a collection of princely ordinances issued with a specific aim. The compilation and the promulgation of these ordinances must have been caused, at least to a certain extent, by the growing opposition to the princely authority both in the city of Kiev and in some country districts. And, indeed, serious riots had occurred in Kiev in 1068. As a result, the eldest of Iaroslav's sons, Iziaslav, Prince of Kiev, was forced to relinquish his throne, if only for a brief period. By issuing their *Pravda*, the princes apparently intended to reënforce their authority so as to avoid the possibility of any repetition of the events of 1068.

Let us now turn to the Expanded Version. It may be divided into three parts: (1) the revised *Pravda* of Iaroslav's sons; (2) the Statute of Vladimir Monomach; and (3) other enactments.

The revision of the *Pravda* of Iaroslav's sons consisted in a certain systematization of content as well as in the addition of some new materials. Thus, for example, the handicraftsman and woman were inserted in the list of people protected by princely legislation. The section on the master of the stables may enable us better to understand the methods of the editorial work of the compilers of the *Pravda*. Sometime between 1054 and 1072 Prince Iziaslav of Kiev imposed a double bloodwite, to the amount of 80 *grivna*, on the murderer of his master of the stables at Dorogobuzh. In the text of the *Pravda* of 1072 we find a general enactment concerning the double bloodwite for the murder of the master of the stables accompanied by a reference to Iziaslav's ordinance of Dorogobuzh.²⁴ In the revised *Pravda* of Iaroslav's sons that reference to a specific case has been omitted.²⁵

The promulgation of the Statute of Vladimir Monomach (Prince of Kiev, 1113–1125) in the very beginning of his reign was the result of dramatic events which followed closely the death of Vladimir's predecessor on the Kievan throne. A serious political and social

---

[23] See Notes to the Short Version, pp. 29, 30.
[24] Short Version, Article 23 (p. 31).
[25] Expanded Version, Article 12 (p. 37).

crisis had been in the making long before that. While the three princes—sons of Iaroslav—attempted to curb the popular opposition by issuing, in 1072, special ordinances for the better protection of princely servitors, the situation apparently required a more constructive legislation. Both the middle-class burghers and the owners of medium-sized landed estates suffered from the high rate of interest on loans contracted by them. Laborers and artisans were in an even worse position since they were threatened with virtual enslavement in the case of inability to meet their financial obligations. The explosion came in 1113 when popular riots reached the force of a social revolution in the city of Kiev.[26] Houses of wealthy boyars and merchants were plundered, and popular resentment turned its fury upon the moneylenders, Jews among the others.

Considerable wisdom and quick action were required on the part of the ruler. Vladimir Monomach—then Prince of Pereiaslav—was the only man to whom the various social classes could turn for guidance, and he was invited to assume the throne of Kiev. Vladimir accepted on condition that there be no opposition to any measures, however drastic, that he might consider necessary. He convoked at once a special Council of State to approve his "new deal" program. This program, as expressed in Vladimir's Statute, consisted in limiting the abuses of short-term loans, limiting the interest on long-term loans, and in issuing special enactments to prevent enslavement of indentured laborers and other lower-class workers caught in the financial web of landlords and moneylenders.

Even after the addition to the Russian Law of such an important piece of legislation as Vladimir's Statute, that Law still contained many lacunae. The original *Pravda* dealt chiefly with the court procedure and penal law. In the revised *Pravda* of Iaroslav's sons a few clauses concerning commercial law were inserted, but other aspects of civil law remained as yet outside the legislator's attention. Further additions to the code were therefore necessary. These additional enactments constitute the third part of the Expanded Version. One group of clauses deals with the family and inheritance law. Another covers the juridical nature of slavery. In this latter group an attempt

---

[26] See B. D. Grekov, *Kievskaia Rus'* (4th ed., Moscow & Leningrad, 1944), pp. 296–298; M. Grushevsky (Hrushevsky), *Istoriia Ukrainy-Rusi*, II (2d ed., Lvov, 1905), 109–110; G. Vernadsky, *Political and Diplomatic History of Russia* (Boston, 1936), pp. 63–64.

is made to put certain limits on the spread of slavery by establishing a number of specific requirements to be observed in the process of enslavement.[27]

The insertion of these additional enactments rounded out the contents of the *Pravda*. Simultaneously, the code must have been revised once more *in toto*. The completion of the Expanded Version as a whole may be referred to the second half of the twelfth century; some scholars are even ready to accept the beginning of the thirteenth century as the date of the final revision. In my opinion, however, there are some reasons to connect the completion of the Expanded Version with the reign of Rostislav, originally Prince of Smolensk and later Prince of Kiev (1160–1168). It is noteworthy that the treaty between Smolensk and the German cities, concluded in 1229, contains several clauses borrowed from the Expanded Version of the *Pravda*. Presumably the latter was the base of Smolensk laws, and if so, it might have been familiarized there by Rostislav.

IV

It is to the princely power, as we have seen, that the initiative belonged in the process of the codification of the Russian Law. In contrast, in the Novgorod and Pskov charters of the fourteenth and fifteenth centuries the prince plays a subordinate role. It is the people themselves who, through the city assembly (*veche*), make and approve the law.

The great city of Novgorod was a rival to Kiev from the early ages of Russian history. Situated on the riverway "from the Varangians to the Greeks," Kiev commanded the exit of commercial caravans from Russia southward in the direction of Constantinople. During the age of the Hanseatic League, Novgorod, which stood at the entrance from the Baltic to inner Russia, was the seat of one of the overseas "factories" of the German merchants. From the time of the establishment of the Teutonic Knights in Prussia and the Livonian Order in Latvia, direct overland contact between Novgorod and Pskov on one hand and the Germans on the other likewise became possible. That contact was not always friendly; years of peaceful commercial relations interchanged with periods of war. Alexander Nevsky's famous vic-

---

[27] Expanded Version, Article 110 (p. 54).

tory over German crusaders (1242) was but one of the episodes in the protracted Russo-German struggle.

Novgorod had two faces. It was a city democracy, and it was also the capital of a huge colonial empire controlling vast territories northward to the White Sea and Arctic Ocean and eastward to the Urals. Within this area Novgorod was "the city" (*gorod*), other towns, even such important ones as Pskov, being known merely as "boroughs" (*prigorod,* literally, "by-town"). The supreme authority was vested in the city assembly (*veche*), in which theoretically all Novgorod citizens could take part, but actually only few of the borough inhabitants could be present, especially when the *veche* met on short notice to handle some emergency business. According to the old customs, a unanimous vote was required to make any *veche* decision valid. As a result, when a considerable group of citizens objected to a bill and did not want to withdraw their objections, force was applied by the majority group. Therefore the *veche* meetings were usually lively and often unruly. In case of a deadlock, both parties might appeal to the spiritual head of the Novgorodian democracy—the *vladyka* (archbishop). Thus, the church was able to play a considerable part in the political life of Novgorod. To the Novgorodians, the Cathedral of St. Sophia, built in the eleventh century, symbolized their city, in any case spiritually. From the political angle, they spoke of their city-state. as "Lord (*Gospodin*) Novgorod the Great" or "Sovereign (*Gosudar'*) Novgorod the Great."

The leading officers of the Novgorod administration—the mayor (*posadnik*) and the chiliarch (*tysiatsky*)—were elected by the direct vote of the city assembly. Usually but not necessarily, they were chosen from among the members of wealthy boyar and merchant families. The retired mayors and chiliarchs, together with other prominent boyars, formed the so-called *Gospoda* (House of Lords), which discussed city affairs prior to the meetings of the *veche*. This added an aristocratic touch to the Novgorodian constitution. The monarchical element was represented by the prince, who must be acceptable to the people of Novgorod and who, on assuming his duties, had to take oath not to violate the city's customs. In most cases the prince was also asked to sign a formal contract in which the limits of his authority were clearly defined. In addition to the copies of those contracts, records of the decisions of the *veche* were kept in the city archives.

It was not until the fifteenth century, however, that the Novgorod law was codified, at least in part. By that time the international position of Novgorod had become precarious, since the city was threatened by two rapidly growing states—the Grand Duchy of Moscow on the southeast and the Grandy Duchy of Lithuania on the southwest. For some time Novgorod was able to play the two rivals against one another by entering into agreements with each of them in turn. In any such agreement the rights and prerogatives of the city had to be made perfectly clear, hence the necessity for the codification of the Novgorodian law. In 1456, the Moscow Grand Duke Vasili II approved a "charter" of Novgorod laws and customs. In 1470 the city signed a treaty with Kazimir IV, king of Poland and grand duke of Lithuania, in which that potentate was recognized as the prince of Novgorod, but his authority was curbed by a number of specific provisions. The treaty proved to be an ephemeral one, however, since in the next year war broke out between Novgorod and Moscow. Receiving no support from Kazimir, Novgorodian troops were outmaneuvered and defeated by Grand Duke Ivan III's skillful generals, and the proud city had to sue for peace. Ivan III was a master politician and believed in expanding his authority by gradual moves. He agreed for the time being to guarantee Novgorod's privileges in exchange for recognition as her "Lord."

It was under such circumstances that the Novgorod "charter" of 1471 came into being. Two copies are extant, both incomplete.[28] Even though the charter has been preserved in part only, it constitutes an important piece of medieval Russian legislation and presents an interesting parallel to the Charter of the City of Pskov of which we possess the full text.

V

Pskov, like Novgorod, was one of Russia's oldest cities. And like Novgorod's, her prosperity was based chiefly upon the Baltic trade. Until the middle of the fourteenth century Pskov was not an independent city-state but merely a "borough" of Novgorod. The Pskovians were entitled to take part in the meetings of the Novgorod *veche,* and thus were connected with the partisan strife in that city.

---

[28] For the literature of the Novgorod, Pskov, and Dvina charters see Bibliography at the end of this volume.

Their voice was, however, not strong enough to affect the decisions of the *veche* to an extent sufficient to compel consideration of the specific interests of Pskov commerce. On many occasions the Pskovians complained that Novgorod was selfishly disregarding their city's needs. Eventually, a movement arose in Pskov to bring to an end the subordination to Novgorod. By the middle of the fourteenth century the movement had succeeded. According to the treaty of 1347, the Novgorodians granted independence to Pskov, recognizing it as a "younger brother." After that time the Pskovians themselves referred to their city as "Lord Pskov." The provisions of the treaty were confirmed in 1397.

As an independent city-state, Pskov had her own princes with whom agreements similar to those in Novgorod were concluded. In church affairs she remained subject to the authority of the Archbishop of Novgorod, who was represented in Pskov by a lieutenant. The Pskov church enjoyed, however, a considerable degree of autonomy, the clergy being organized in several "cathedral districts." [29] The main sanctuary of the city was the Holy Trinity Cathedral which enjoyed as much local prestige as did the rival Novgorod Cathedral of St. Sophia.

Like Novgorod, Pskov had to pay much attention to her relations with neighboring states and to the preservation of political equilibrium among them. For a long time the Pskovians were successful in keeping the balance between Novgorod, Moscow, and Lithuania.

The city charter was approved by the assembly after the assertion of Pskov liberties in the treaty with Novgorod of 1397. The charter was expanded and revised by 1467.[30] A fragment of the Pskov charter, from Article 109 to the end, was found by the "historiographer" N. M. Karamzin and published by him in the notes to Volume V of his great work, *Istoriia Gosudarstva Rossiiskogo* (1816). Later, a complete copy was discovered in the private archives of Count Vorontsov by Professor Murzakevich, who published it in 1847.

VI

We now turn to the Charter of Dvina Land. Dvina Land was the name for the territory in the basin of the Northern Dvina River cen-

---

[29] See the Charter of the City of Pskov, Preamble note, p. 61.
[30] *Ibid.*, notes, pp. 61, 62.

tering around the towns of Vologda and Ustiug. This remote northern country was at the junction of two important commercial ways, one leading from Novgorod eastward to the Urals, and the other northward from Moscow to the White Sea. The country was abundant in forests and rich in fur-bearing animals. Even in the fourteenth century hunting was so profitable an occupation that people paid their taxes in furs. However, commerce and agriculture also played an important role in the Land's economy.

Dvina Land was a Novgorod Dominion from at least the eleventh century. By the fourteenth century, however, the boyars and wealthy merchants of the region, although Novgorod citizens, were dissatisfied with the policies of the Novgorod *veche*. In their opinion, Novgorod treated their Land as a colony, demanding excessive taxes and neglecting local interests. They therefore turned to the Grand Dukes of Moscow for protection, in the hope of striking a better bargain with them. In 1397, when an uprising against the Novgorodian rule occurred in Dvina Land, Muscovite troops seized the opportunity to enter the territory. Anxious to secure the loyalty of the Dvina people, Grand Duke Vasili I of Moscow issued a special charter to guarantee the autonomy of local courts and administration.

The Muscovite intervention proved to be premature and in the next year the Novgorodian authority was reëstablished in Dvina Land. Vasili's charter, although of short duration, presents an interesting legal document. The text of the Dvina charter was first published by N. M. Karamzin in 1818.

VII

In conclusion, a few words about the principles of the translation of the medieval Russian documents for this volume would not be amiss. Translation is never an easy work, and the degree of its success is always a comparative one. No translation, however adequate, can ever replace the original. Every translator is faced with at least two dangers: either, in the effort to keep close to the original, he correctly translates single words but fails to render the spirit and thereby fails to make the general meaning of the original sufficiently clear; or, if his predilection is toward general meaning, he is inclined to take too great liberties with the text, and the result is then, more often than not, a paraphrase, not a translation.

In translating a novel or a play, a good paraphrase may be a better solution than the clumsy conveyance of so many words from one language into another. In translations of historical and juridical sources, however, an emphasis on either of these methods of approach may be equally fatal; the golden mean must be sought at any cost. In the case of medieval documents the specific difficulties are even greater, since some of the terms and constructions used in an old language do not correspond to those in the modern language. What matters even more, our very ways of life and thought have changed to such an extent since the Middle Ages that we may not always be sure of understanding properly the reality which lies behind the words of the text.

Translating Russian medieval documents is certainly no easier than translating similar material in German, French, or any other language. And the *Pravda Russkaia,* in particular, is fraught with riddles. There is almost no single Article in the *Pravda* which has not been variously interpreted by different scholars. In order to cope with these problems with any reasonable expectation of success, it is essential for the translator to try to familiarize himself not only with the old Russian language but with the peculiarities of the style of the old Russian jurists as well as with their mentality.

Moreover, with all due reservations, the *Pravda* is not a systematic code in our sense; it consists mostly of casual juridical notes and comments rather than of comprehensive definitions. It has a logic of its own, which we must discover. The compilers of the document addressed themselves not so much to the general public as to the judges and court officials. It was assumed that the latter were thoroughly familiar with the whole body of the customary law and needed only some supplementary information concerning new ordinances. As a result, there are logical lacunae in almost every clause of the document. What has not been said is often as important for our understanding of the text as what is said. Obviously, for rightly interpreting the text we must somehow make up the deficit in wording in order to obtain a more or less adequate idea of what the compiler meant. The best way to fill in the gaps—logical or literary—is by analogy with similar clauses in other parts of the same code or in other contemporary sources. If this is not possible, one has chiefly to rely upon a minute analysis of the economic and social conditions by which the clause in question may have been conditioned; under-

INTRODUCTION 23

standing these may help to clarify the interpretation. Unfortunately our knowledge of Kievan economics is still far from adequate and such an approach cannot always promise success.

The present translator has tried to do all this preliminary work; accordingly, each clause is translated without bothering the reader with the process of argumentation. In some cases, however, it seemed indispensable to supply at least part of the phrase implied but not expressed in the text. This supplementary material is enclosed in brackets.

The treatment of specific juridical and social terms presented another problem by itself. There still exists no consensus of opinion among scholars about some of them. The easiest method would have been not to translate such terms but merely to transliterate them, in each case explaining the connotation in the notes. This would, however, result in a text littered with Russian terms in italics and would also mean shifting the responsibility from the translator to the reader. Therefore, the opposite method has been adopted, that of translating each Russian term into the closest possible equivalent in modern English and, for the original term, referring the reader to the notes. Thus, the reader will find in the text only English terms, such as, for example, "bailiff" and "peasant"; he will have to look in the notes, if he is eager to know the original Russian terms (in the present example, *ognishchanin* and *smerd*, respectively). The only exception to the rule is the term *izgoi* which I have left untranslated in the text, explaining it in the notes. This was necessary because the connotation of the term as used in the *Pravda* must have been entirely different from the usual one, and, although I have an explanation for it, I did not consider it proper to impose my conjecture on the reader.

Furthermore, for obvious reasons, the names of the Russian monetary units could not be rendered into English. Nor would it be expedient to explain the value of each unit in the notes separately, since the reader needs first of all some general information on medieval Russian money and monetary system, without which the value of a specific unit could not be understood. Therefore, it seems proper to insert herewith a brief note on Russian money in the period of the *Pravda* as well as in that of the Pskov and Novgorod charters.

Since furs constituted in the early periods an important item of Russian commerce—as they were to do in Siberia in the sixteenth and the seventeenth centuries—it was but natural that furs may have played, at least in some periods and in some districts, the role of currency. However, Russian commerce with Byzantium and the East also brought to Russia gold and silver in considerable amounts, and while, in the Kievan period, the common Russian word for "money" was *kuny* (marten skins), the Russian monetary system—or rather systems, since there were several of them—was based on metal rather than on fur.

The basic monetary unit, in the Kievan period, was the *grivna*. There were three kinds of *grivna:* gold, silver, and *kuna*. It is not always easy to determine which kind is meant in a given article of the Russian Law. The gold *grivna* presumably corresponded to one half a troy pound of gold. The silver *grivna* must have equaled approximately one troy pound of silver. The gold *grivna* was seldom used. The silver *grivna* was a standard unit in all commercial transactions and particularly in foreign trade.

In the payments of taxes and fines of smaller amount, as well as in other every-day species transactions, the reckoning was in *grivna* of *kuna*. Fractions of this were known as *nogata* and *rezana*. There were 20 *nogata* and 50 *rezana* in one *grivna* of *kuna*. The lowest unit was known as *veksha* (literally, squirrel) or *veveritsa;* in Smolensk, one *nogata* was equal to 24 *veksha*. Somewhat later, the term *kuna* in the specific sense of a fraction of *grivna* was introduced. There is no consensus of scholarly opinion about the exact value of one *kuna* in relation to one *grivna* of *kuna*. According to Prozorovsky, there were 50 *kuna* in a *grivna*, which would mean that one *kuna* was equal to one *rezana*. However, according to Mrochek-Drozdovsky, there must have been 25 *kuna* in one *grivna* of *kuna*, making one *kuna* equal to two *rezana*. As to the relation between the silver *grivna* and the *grivna* of *kuna*, it is known that in Smolensk one silver *grivna* was considered equal to four *grivna* of *kuna*. It may be mentioned furthermore that in chronicles as well as in some other sources, one more term for money occurs: *bela*. It is hard to say whether this was a general word for a silver coin, or a term denoting a specific monetary unit.

While both the silver *grivna* and the *grivna* of *kuna* were still in use in Novgorod and Pskov as late as the fourteenth and fifteenth centuries, a new monetary unit, called "ruble," gradually assumed predominance. The word "ruble" (*rubl'*) is usually considered a derivation from the Russian verb *rubiti* ("to cut"); ruble is supposed to have originated from cutting a *grivna* into four pieces.[31] In my opinion, however, *rubl'* is the Russian spelling of *rūpya* which, in Sanskrit, means "silver."[32] A Novgorodian ruble corresponded originally to a silver *grivna*. In the fifteenth century the ruble amounted to only one half of a silver *grivna*. The Novgorodian ruble of the fifteenth century was equal to 216 *denga*. In Pskov they counted 220 *denga* to the ruble; in Moscow, 100 *denga*. *Denga* is a term borrowed from the Mongolian language.

And now, let the documents speak for themselves.

---

[31] See L. Wanstrat, *Beiträge zur Charakteristik des russischen Wortschatzes* (Leipzig, 1933), p. 14.

[32] See N. Stchoupak, L. Nitti, and L. Renou, *Dictionnaire sanskrit-français* (Paris, 1932), p. 608.

THE RUSSIAN LAW

A. THE SHORT VERSION
[I. Iaroslav's Pravda]

ARTICLE 1. If a man kills a man [the following relatives of the murdered man may avenge him]: the brother is to avenge his brother; the son, his father; or the father, his son; and the son of the brother [of the murdered man] or the son of his sister, [their respective uncle]. If there is no avenger, [the murderer pays] 40 *grivna* wergeld. Be [the murdered man] a [Kievan] Russian— a palace guard, a merchant, an agent, or a sheriff—be he an *Izgoi*, or a [Novgorodian] Slav, his wergeld is 40 *grivna*.

THE SHORT VERSION. Grekov's edition of the Academy copy of the Short Version has been used for this translation. The division into articles is Grekov's.

ARTICLE 1. The old custom of blood revenge is here limited by the prince's authority in so far that a precise list of the relatives entitled to avenge a murder is offered. "Man," *muzh*. The term *muzh* is used in old Russian both in a general sense ("any man") and in a more specific sense, besides its connotation "husband." *Muzh* in a specific social sense is a man of noble origin, or of a high social position, a "knight"; here it contrasts with *liudin*, another old Russian word denoting "man" (see note to Article 3, p. 36). In the list of categories of men worth normal wergeld, which forms the second half of Article 1, the Russian term *iabetnik* has been translated as "agent"; it corresponds to *umbodsmadr* in Norwegian laws (Larson, *The Earliest Norwegian Laws*, p. 409); in old Swedish *oembete* means "office," "service." Sheriff, *mechnik*; in other texts, *metelnik*. The term *mechnik* is usually explained as "swordsman," from *mech*, sword. Metelnik derives from *metati*, literally, "to throw," "to cast," but also, in old Russian, "to launch," "to administer." In my opinion both of these terms should be derived from *metati*. It must be said, however, that Louise Wanstrat derives *metelnik* from the old Low German word *metal*, a technical term denoting that part of the composition which goes to certain relatives of the murdered man (see L. Wanstrat, *Beiträge zur Charakteristik des russischen Wortschatzes*, Leipzig, 1933, p. 94).

The connotation of the term *izgoi* is one of the moot problems of medieval Russian law. It has been suggested that the *izgoi* must have been a man who broke with his guild, or his clan. In the twelfth-century sources, *izgoi* is used

THE SHORT VERSION

ARTICLE 2. If [a man injures a man, and the injured man] is smeared with blood or is blue from bruises, he needs no eyewitness [to prove the offense]; if there is no mark [of injury] upon him, let him produce an eyewitness; if he cannot, the matter ends there. If he is not able to avenge, he receives 3 *grivna* for the offense and the physician receives his honorarium.

ARTICLE 3. If anyone hits another with a club, or a rod, or a fist, or a bowl, or a [drinking] horn, or the butt [of a tool or of a vessel], and [the offender] evades being hit [in his turn], he [the offender] has to pay 12 *grivna* and that ends the matter.

ARTICLE 4. If [anyone] strikes [another] with a sword without unsheathing it, or with the hilt of a sword, 12 *grivna* for the offense.

ARTICLE 5. If [anyone] cuts [another's] arm, and the arm is cut off or shrinks, 40 *grivna*.

ARTICLE 6. If [anyone cuts another's leg and] the leg is cut off, or the [injured man] becomes lame, then the latter's sons have to chastise [the offender].

ARTICLE 7. If a finger is cut off, 3 *grivna* for the offense.

ARTICLE 8. And for the mustache, 12 *grivna*; and for the beard, 12 *grivna*.

ARTICLE 9. He who unsheathes his sword, but does not strike, pays one *grivna*.

ARTICLE 10. If a man pulls a man toward himself or pushes him, 3 *grivna*, but [the offended man] has to bring two eyewitnesses; [however] in case he is a Varangian, or a Kolbiag, an oath is to be taken.

---

in the sense of a freedman working on the church or princely domains. It is obvious, however, that in this clause of the Russian Law the term must mean something different, since *izgoi* here is being guaranteed full wergeld. In my opinion, *izgoi* may denote here a member of princely retinue of Ossetian or Circassian origin; see G. Vernadsky, "Three Notes on the Social History of Kievan Russia," *Slavonic and East European Review*, XXII (1944), pp. 88–92.

ARTICLE 2. Eyewitness, in Russian, *vidok*, an archaic term peculiar to the Novgorod dialect. See Introduction, Section II (p. 11), on the difference between the role of an "eyewitness" (*vidok*) and that of a "witness" (*poslukh*) in the medieval Russian court procedure.

ARTICLE 10. The oath (*rotá*) mentioned here is part of the court procedure; it was accepted, under certain circumstances, as judicial evidence (see Introduction, Section II, p. 11). The exemption from the normal

ARTICLE 11. If a slave runs away from a Varangian or a Kolbiag and [the man who conceals that slave] does not declare him for three days, and [the owner] discovers him on the third day, he [the owner] receives his slave back and 3 *grivna* for the offense.

ARTICLE 12. If anyone rides another's horse without asking the owner's permission, he has to pay 3 *grivna*.

ARTICLE 13. If anyone takes another's horse, or weapon, or clothes, and [the owner] identifies [the object] within his township, he receives it back and 3 *grivna* for the offense.

ARTICLE 14. If the owner identifies [his property outside of his town] he must not seize it outright; do not tell [the man who holds

---

court procedure, here and in some other clauses of the Russian Law, in regard to the Varangian or the Kolbiag is to be explained by the fact that either of these terms refers to a foreigner who has no close contact with local people. The presumption is in this case that it might be difficult for a Varangian or a Kolbiag to produce eyewitnesses. The term Kolbiag has been explained by various scholars in different ways—as a Scandinavian, a Baltic Slav, a Lithuanian, or a Turkic tribesman. It is known that one of the Patzinak tribes was called Kulpa. Lately Max Vasmer has come to the conclusion that the name Kolbiag corresponds to that of a North German clan, Kylfingar; see his articles, "Beiträge zur Slavischen Altertumskunde, VII, Die Kylfingar in Russland," *Zeitschrift für Slavische Philologie*, VIII (1931), pp. 120–124, and "Wikingerspuren in Russland," *Sitzungsberichte der preussischen Akademie der Wissenschaften, Phil.-Hist. Klasse*, XXIV (1931), 10, 11. See also Gyula Moravcsik, *Byzantinoturcica*, II (Budapest, 1943), 148.

ARTICLE 11. My interpretation of this clause differs from the one usually accepted, according to which the Varangian or the Kolbiag would be here not the owner of the runaway slave but the defendant in the case—the man who conceals the slave. While conceding that the text is not quite clear I am convinced of the validity of my interpretation. The case is apparently that of a slave running away from a foreign merchant who bought him, before the merchant's departure for his homeland.

ARTICLE 12. This clause is similar to the second part of Article 24 of the *Zakon Sudnyi Liudem*, a Bulgarian law manual of the tenth century (see Saturnik, p. 150).

ARTICLE 13. By "township," the Russian term *mir* is rendered here. It means any kind of local community. *Verv'* (guild) in Article 20, Short Version, as well as in articles 3–8, Expanded Version, is an association of neighbors in a country district. See note to Article 20, below.

ARTICLE 14. "Confrontment," in Russian, *svod*. This institution is a peculiar feature of the old Russian examination procedure. See Introduction, Section II (pp. 10, 11).

the property]: "This is mine," but tell him thus: "Come for confrontation to the place where you got it"; and if he does not come immediately he must produce two bails [to guarantee that he will come] within five days.

ARTICLE 15. If a man [engaged in business] claims his share in the balance from his partner, and the latter balks, he has to go for an investigation by [a jury of] 12 men; if [it is established] that he [the partner] maliciously refused to refund [the first man's share], the man must receive his money and 3 *grivna* for the offense.

ARTICLE 16. If anyone, having recognized his [runaway] slave [in another's possession] wants to take him, [the man who holds that slave] has to lead [the owner] to the party from whom he bought that slave, and that party has to lead [the owner] to the one [from whom he bought the slave], and [so they go eventually] even to the third party. Then tell the third party: "Give me the slave, and sue [the fourth party] for your money with [the help of] an eyewitness."

ARTICLE 17. And if a slave strikes a freeman and hides in [his master's] house, and his master is not willing to give him up, the master has to pay 12 *grivna*, and the offended freeman beats the slave whenever he finds him.

ARTICLE 18. And if anyone breaks [another's] spear, or shield, or [cuts his] clothes and wants to keep them, he must pay for them. And if he wants to return the damaged things he has to pay for the damage.

[II. THE PRAVDA OF IAROSLAV'S SONS]

[PREAMBLE]. The Law of the Russian land enacted when [the princes] Iziaslav, Vsevolod, Sviatoslav, [and their councilors]

ARTICLES 16 and 17. While both of these sections deal with the slave, the Russian term for "slave" is different in each case: in Article 16 an older term, *cheliadin* is used; in Article 17, a more recent term, *kholop*. Article 17 is obviously a later interpolation, to be compared with Article 65 of the Expanded Version (pp. 47, 48).

ARTICLE 18. There is a great similarity between this clause and Article 75 of the *Zakon Sudnyi Liudem* (see Saturnik, p. 163).

PREAMBLE TO THE PRAVDA OF IAROSLAV'S SONS. Iaroslav died in 1054 after having divided his realm between his sons, of whom the three elder— Iziaslav, prince of Kiev; Sviatoslav, prince of Chernigov; and Vsevolod,

Kosniachko, Pereneg, Mikyfor the Kievan, Chudin, and Mikula met together.

ARTICLE 19. If they kill the bailiff, deliberately, the [actual] murderer has to pay 80 *grivna* [as bloodwite], and the guild is not liable. And for the prince's adjutant, 80 *grivna*.

prince of Pereiaslav—established a kind of triumvirate. The conference mentioned here took place, presumably, in 1072 (see Introduction, Section III, pp. 14, 15). One may notice that the order of names of the princes in the Preamble (Iziaslav, Vsevolod, Sviatoslav) does not correspond to the natural order of their seniority (Iziaslav, Sviatoslav, Vsevolod), in which they were undoubtedly listed in the original minutes of the conference. Apparently at some time the original text of the preamble was changed. When and under what circumstances did that change occur? In 1073 the second brother, Sviatoslav, ousted Iziaslav from Kiev and occupied his throne. It was only after Sviatoslav's death that Iziaslav returned to Kiev where he reigned, for the second time, until his death (1076–1078), to be succeeded on the throne of Kiev by the third brother, Vsevolod. Presumably, it is in the period of Iziaslav's second reign in Kiev that the order of names of the princes was changed in Iziaslav's copy of the preamble. At that time Vsevolod was next to Iziaslav as his successor-designate, and moreover, Sviatoslav—then already dead—must have been regarded as an usurper who forfeited his seniority by his illegal seizure of Kiev in 1073. It may be added that Vsevolod (Prince of Kiev, 1078–1093) was extremely popular among the clergy and was therefore given prominent place in the chronicles. Thus, once his name was given the second ranking in the preamble of the Short Version, it was willingly kept there by later copyists. Turning now to the other members of the meeting, Kosniachko is mentioned in the "Book of Annals" under 1068, as a general (*voevoda*). Mikyfor is the South Russian (Ukrainian) spelling of the name Nikifor (Nicephorus). "Nikifor's house" in Kiev is mentioned in the "Book of Annals." Furthermore, according to a Life of S. S. Boris and Gleb, Chudin was the governor of Vyshgorod in 1072; Nikola (Mikula) is mentioned in the same Life as the chairman of the guild of the carpenters—builders of bridges and town walls—at Vyshgorod.

ARTICLE 19. This clause, as well as the following ones (down to Article 27), establishes a scale of bloodwite payments and fines for the murder of various princely officials as well as for that of men and women working for the prince or dependent on him in one way or another. These clauses derive from the general principle of the legislation of Iaroslav's sons, that is, the abolishment of blood revenge and the introduction of the bloodwite payments instead (see Article 2, p. 35). Two prince's officials are specifically mentioned in this section: *ognishchanin* (bailiff) and *podiezdnoi* (messenger, or adjutant). The term *ognishchanin* is to be derived from *ognishche*

ARTICLE 20. And if the bailiff is killed in a highway attack and they do not search for the murderers, that guild within the boundaries of which the body has been found has to pay the bloodwite.

ARTICLE 21. And if, while stealing cows, they murder the bailiff near a barn, or near a horse [stable] or a cow [shed], [the one who murders the bailiff] is to be killed like a dog. This also refers to [the case of the murder of] the assistant steward.

ARTICLE 22. And for the prince's steward, 80 *grivna*.

ARTICLE 23. And for the master of the stable 80 *grivna*, as constituted by Iziaslav in the case of his master of the stable whom the Dorogobuzhians killed.

ARTICLE 24. And for [the murder of] the prince's farm manager as well as of the field overseer, 12 *grivna*.

(hearth). As may be seen from Article 21 below, *ognishchanin* is the general manager of princely estates.

ARTICLE 20. This is a clause establishing the principle of collective responsibility of the members of the guild (*verv'*) for the murder committed within its boundaries. In regard to its function here the *verv'* is comparable to a frith-gild in Anglo-Saxon law as well as to a frank-pledge group in medieval England. See Articles 3-8 of the Expanded Version.

ARTICLE 21. This article is famous in the annals of Russian legal history for the protracted controversy concerning its meaning. The text, at first glance, seems indeed ambiguous. In reading it without due attention to the peculiarities of the old Russian juridical style one may wonder whether it is an outside thief or the bailiff himself who is supposed to be caught stealing cows and to be killed like a dog for the offense. A number of scholars, including L. K. Goetz, considered the bailiff himself the thief in this case. Such interpretation is utterly misleading. The clause obviously deals with a double crime: stealing cows and killing the bailiff when the latter tried to prevent the theft. If the thief-murderer be subsequently caught by the bailiff's assistants he is to be killed "like a dog," that is, the bailiff's assistants bear no responsibility for his murder. Compare Article 38, p. 33, and Article 40, p. 41.

ARTICLE 22. "Steward," *tivun* or *tiun*, from the old Swedish *thiun* "servant." Originally the prince's (or the boyar's) steward, *tiun* later became the princely judge. One may note that in the Expanded Version the term *ognishchanin* is replaced by that of *tiun ognishchny*. "Assistant steward," mentioned in the preceding section, *tivunets*.

ARTICLE 23. "Master of the stable," *koniukh stary* ("the senior groom"); in the Expanded Version, Article 12, *tiun koniushii* ("the steward of grooms").

ARTICLE 25. And for the contract laborer on princely estates, 5 *grivna*.

ARTICLE 26. And for a peasant, or a herdsman, 5 *grivna*.

ARTICLE 27. And for the slave tutor or nurse, 12 *grivna*.

ARTICLE 28. And for a horse with prince's brand, 3 *grivna*, and for the peasant's horse, 2 *grivna;* for a mare, 60 *rezana;* for an ox, one *grivna;* for a cow, 40 *rezana;* and for a three-year-old [cow], 15 *kuna;* and for a yearling [heifer], a half *grivna;* and for a calf, 5 *rezana;* and for a yearling ewe, one *nogata,* and for a [yearling] ram, one *nogata.*

ARTICLE 29. And if anyone abducts another man's male or female slave, he has to pay 12 *grivna* for the offense.

ARTICLE 30. If there comes a man smeared with blood or blue from bruises he needs no witness [to prove the offense].

ARTICLE 31. And if they steal horses or oxen or [some property in the] barn, and if it was the work of one man only, he has to pay

---

ARTICLE 25. "Contract laborer," *riadovnich;* in other texts, *riadovich,* from *riad,* agreement, contract.

ARTICLE 26. "And for a *smerd,* or for a *khop,* five *grivna.*" I have interpreted *smerd* as "peasant," and *khop* as "herdsman." The *smerdy* (which is plural from *smerd*) were peasants whose legal status was somewhat limited by the princely authority although they were freemen. In my opinion the term *smerd* derives from the Iranian *mard* (man). The case of *khop* is much more difficult. The term is usually explained as a misspelling for *kholop* (slave); and indeed in the corresponding article of the Archaeographic Commission copy of the Short Version as well as in Article 16 of the Expanded Version we read not *khop* but *kholop.* However, we have to handle old texts with every care and consideration and to resort to emendation only if there is no other way of explaining the term. In 1939 Dr. A. Efron offered a new explanation of the term *khop,* and while I would take exception to some points in his argumentation, I am ready to accept his conclusion that *khop* means "herdsman" in this case. In my opinion *khop* is a herdsman of Patzinak extraction. One may recall that, according to Constantine Porphyrogenitus, one of the Patzinak tribes was called Khop. (See G. Vernadsky, "Three Notes," *Slav. and E. Europ. Review,* XXII [1944], pp. 85–88.) To complicate the issue even more, in the Archaeographic Commission copy of the Short Version, as well as in Article 16 of the Expanded Version, the clause reads not "for a peasant, or for a slave 5 *grivna,*" but "for the peasant's slave, 5 *grivna*" (*v smerd'i v kholopi,* Arch. Comm.; *za smerdii kholop,* Article 16, Expanded Version). For this reason, some scholars have suggested that Article 26 of the Short Version, as well as Article 16 of the Expanded Version, deals with the case of the

[three] *grivna* and 30 *rezana;* and if there were [as many as] 18 robbers, each pays three *grivna* and 30 *rezana.*

ARTICLE 32. And if they burn or break a prince's beehive, 3 *grivna.*

ARTICLE 33. And if they inflict pain on a peasant without the prince's order, 3 *grivna* for the offense; and for the bailiff, and for the assistant steward, and the sheriff, 12 *grivna.*

ARTICLE 34. And if anyone plows beyond the bound [of his property] or beyond a hedge, 12 *grivna* for the offense.

ARTICLE 35. And if anyone steals a boat, he has to pay 30 *rezana* for the boat and a fine of 60 *rezana.*

ARTICLE 36. And for a dove or a fowl, 9 *kuna;* and for a duck, or a goose, or a crane, or a swan, 30 *rezana;* and a fine of 60 *rezana.*

ARTICLE 37. And if they steal another man's hound or hawk, or falcon, 3 *grivna* for the offense.

ARTICLE 38. And if they kill a thief in their own yard, or at the barn, or at the stable, he is [rightly] killed; but if they hold him until daylight, they have to bring him to the prince's court; and in case [they hold him until daylight and then] kill him, and people have seen him bound [before he was killed], they have to pay for him.

ARTICLE 39. If they steal hay, 9 *kuna;* and for lumber, 9 *kuna.*

ARTICLE 40. If they steal a ewe, or a goat, or a sow, and ten people were [in the gang], each pays a fine of 60 *rezana;* and he who rescued [the ewe], receives 10 *rezana.*

ARTICLE 41. And from each [three] *grivna* [of fines collected] one *kuna* is paid to the sheriff; 15 *kuna* goes [to the church] as tithe; and the prince receives three *grivna.* And from 12 *grivna* the sheriff

---

murder of a peasant's slave only, and not at all with that of a peasant. This explanation was welcomed by scholars who doubted that the penalty for the murder of a *smerd*—a freeman—could be equal to the penalty for the murder of a slave (*kholop*). But, as has just been mentioned, the legal status of the *smerdy* was somewhat limited. Moreover, 5 *grivna* for the murder of a *smerd* represent only the fine to the prince, besides which an amend was to be paid to the murdered smerd's relatives; and 5 *grivna* paid for the murder of the prince's slave ended the case.

ARTICLE 35. "Fine" (payable to the prince), *prodazha.*

ARTICLES 41 and 42. These two articles form really a separate statute attached to the original *Pravda.* It deals with the distribution of the collected bloodwite payments between the prince, his officials, and the church (Ar-

receives 70 *kuna;* [the church], two *grivna* as tithe; and the prince, 10 *grivna.*

ARTICLE 42. And [when the bloodwite collector and his assistants are on their journey for collecting fines, they receive provisions from the population] according to custom, as follows: the collector receives 7 buckets of malt, and a sheep or a portion [of a beef], or two *nogata* for one week; and on Wednesday, one *rezana* or [the equivalent in] curd; and on Friday, the same; and as much bread as they can eat, and millet; and two hens a day; and [they have the right] to put up 4 horses in the stable, and [the owner of the stable] has to give the horses as much [oats] as they can eat. And the bloodwite collector receives 60 *grivna,* and 10 *rezana,* and 12 *veveritsa* [of which] one *grivna* in advance. And if [the collection drive] occurs during Lent, [then the food is fish] and [he receives] 7 *rezana* for fish. Thus, they receive 15 *kuna* a week in cash, and as much food as they can eat; [but in each locality] they have to complete the collection of the bloodwite within a week. Such is Iaroslav's ordinance.

ARTICLE 43. And this is the table of payments for the builders of bridges: when they complete the bridge, they receive one *nogata* for

---

ticle 41), and with the amount of provisions to be supplied by the local people to the bloodwite collector (*virnik*) during his traveling about the country for the collection of bloodwite payments (Article 42). It has been suggested that this table of supplies was originally issued in 1036 by Prince Iaroslav to the people of Novgorod for their protection against any excessive claims of the officials. It is to be noted that this statute is the only passage in the whole *Pravda* where a direct influence of the church is felt. In Article 41 the tithe is mentioned, and in Article 42 fish diet is recommended during Lent. Russia was officially converted to Christianity only in 988, and in the first half of the eleventh century Lent was not yet as generally observed as it was later on. The clergy missed no opportunity to impose the habit of fasting on the people. For these reasons we may infer that either the Bishop of Novgorod or his deputy was among the editors of this statute.

In regard to Article 41 it must be said that its text seems to have been mutilated by copyists, since there is some confusion in the figures. According to Vladimirsky-Budanov, not one but 15 *kuna* was to be paid to the sheriff. Thus, instead of 3 *grivna,* the amount of 3 *grivna* and 30 *kuna* (15 *kuna* to the sheriff and 15 *kuna* to the church) was supposed to be actually collected in this case, which means that fees to the sheriff and a tithe to the church were added to the original amount of fines.

ARTICLE 43. This clause likewise represents a separate enactment. Its insertion in the code may have been the result of the advice of Mikula, the

their work and one *nogata* for lumber [for each span of the bridge]. And if they have to repair several planks of an old bridge—three, or four, or five—they are paid accordingly.

B. THE EXPANDED VERSION

[I. THE REVISED *Pravda* OF IAROSLAV'S SONS]

THE ORDINANCES OF IAROSLAV, SON OF VLADIMIR

ARTICLE 1. If a man kills a man [the following relatives of the murdered man may avenge him]: the brother is to avenge his brother, or the father, [his son], or the son, [his father]; or the son of the brother, or the son of the sister, [their respective uncle]. If there is no avenger the wergeld is set to the amount of 80 *grivna* in case [the murdered man] was a prince's councilor or a prince's steward; if he was a [Kievan] Russian—a palace guard, a merchant, or a boyar's steward, or a sheriff—or if he was an *Izgoi*, or a [Novgorodian] Slav, [the wergeld is] 40 *grivna*.

ARTICLE 2. And after Iaroslav his sons: Iziaslav, Sviatoslav, and Vsevolod, and their councilors: Kosniachko, Pereneg, and Nikifor met in a conference and canceled the [custom] of blood revenge, and [instead ordered] composition of [the crime] by money. And as to anything else, all that Iaroslav had decreed, his sons confirmed accordingly.

---

chairman of the guild of carpenter-builders (see note to Preamble, p. 30, above). In old Russian, "bridge" (*most*) means not only a structure erected over a river but also a timber pavement of city streets. In northern cities like Novgorod and Pskov, where the ground was swampy and wood plentiful, it was usual to pave the main thoroughfares with wood blocks.

THE EXPANDED VERSION. Grekov's edition of the Trinity copy of the Expanded Version has been used for translation. The division into articles is Grekov's, except that for the sake of convenience, his Article 45 has been subdivided into Articles 45 and 45A; and Article 53 into Articles 53 and 53A.

ARTICLE 1. Comparing this with Article 1 of the Short Version we notice that instead of a single wergeld of 40 *grivna*, two classes of wergeld are now established: a double wergeld of 80 *grivna* for the prince's high officials, and the normal wergeld of 40 *grivna* for other categories.

ARTICLE 2. This is obviously not a formal clause but a note on the enactment of Iaroslav's sons. Comparing it with the preamble to the *Pravda* of Iaroslav's sons, in the Short Version, we notice that the names of the three

On Homicide

ARTICLE 3. If anyone kills a prince's man in a highway attack, and the [local people] do not search for the murderer, the guild within the territory where the body lies has to pay the bloodwite [which, for the prince's official, is] 80 *grivna*, and for a commoner, 40 *grivna*.

ARTICLE 4. And if a guild has to pay a "dark" bloodwite, its members [are allowed] to pay [in installments] for several years, since they pay on behalf of [an unknown] murderer.

ARTICLE 5. If the murderer appears within the guild [after the payments of the "dark" bloodwite have been already started], let him pay the balance, since they [the members of the guild] had helped him by starting payments of the "dark" bloodwite. But in any case they shall together pay 40 *grivna* [as bloodwite] in full; and as to the bot, it is only the murderer who pays it; and he pays his share of the 40 *grivna* [bloodwite].

ARTICLE 6. And if [a man] kills [a man] publicly in a brawl or at a feast he likewise shall pay his share in the guild's liabilities.

Concerning [the Man] Who Kills [Another Man] in an Attack without Provocation

ARTICLE 7. And if [a man] kills [a man] in an attack without provocation, the [members of the guild] do not pay for the murderer but surrender him with his wife and children for banishment and confiscation of his property.

ARTICLE 8. And to one who fails to assume his share in [the payments of] the "dark" bloodwite, the members of the guild give no help but he has to pay [everything] himself.

---

princes are here listed in the natural order of their seniority. Presumably, the editors of the Expanded Version had access to the original copy of the preamble to the Pravda of Iaroslav's sons in the Short Version, or to a copy of the minutes of the meeting. On the other hand, out of the five princely councilors mentioned in the preamble to the Short Version only three are listed here.

ARTICLE 3. "Prince's man," *kniazh muzh*; "commoner," *liudin*. For the interrelation of the terms *muzh* and *liudin*, see note to Article 1, Short Version (p. 26).

ARTICLES 3–8. These clauses establish, under certain circumstances, collective responsibility of the members of the guild within the boundaries of

ARTICLE 9. And the customary food rations of the bloodwite collector under Iaroslav are as follows: the bloodwite collector receives 7 buckets of malt and a sheep or a portion [of a beef], or 2 *nogata* for one week; and on Wednesday one *kuna* or [the equivalent in] curd; and on Friday the same; and two hens a day; and 7 loaves of bread for a week; and 7 measures of millet; and 7 measures of peas; and 7 bricks of salt. This is to the bloodwite collector with his clerk. And oats for 4 horses. And the bloodwite collector receives 8 *grivna*, and 10 *kuna* for traveling expenses; and the sheriff receives 12 *veksha*. And the arrival [welcome] money is 1 *grivna*.

ARTICLE 10. When the bloodwite is 80 *grivna*, the collector receives 16 *grivna* and 10 *kuna* and 12 *veksha;* and the arrival [welcome] money *grivna* in advance, and 3 *grivna* head money.

Concerning the Prince's Officials

ARTICLE 11. And [the wergeld] of the prince's page, or groom, or [man] cook is 40 *grivna*.

ARTICLE 12. And for the palace steward and the stable steward, 80 *grivna*.

---

which a murder has been committed. The bloodwite (*vira*) to be paid by the members of the guild collectively is here called *dikaia vira;* in some of the other manuscripts, however, this kind of bloodwite is called *liudskaia vira*. The Russian adjective *dikii*, of which *dikaia* is the feminine form, means "wild"; in Old Russian it also had a connotation of "gray." I understand it as "dark," since the term was apparently first applied to the cases when the murderer was unknown. Later it was extended to all kinds of collectively paid bloodwite. The adjective *liudskoi* (*liudskaia* is the feminine form) means "of the people" and derives from *liudin*, man, plural *liudi*. *Liudskaia vira* means "bloodwite paid by men," that is, collectively. Goetz suggested that *dikaia vira* is a corruption of *liudskaia vira*. This latter term he interpreted as "man-bot" (Manbusse, *leodgeld*). His theory seems ingenious at first glance, but is faulty nevertheless. First, the term *dikaia vira* occurs not only in the Russian Law but in some other sources as well. Thus, it is not a corruption of *liudskaia vira*, but a parallel term. Secondly, *vira* means "bloodwite," and not "bot." Thirdly, *liudskaia vira* is not "man-bloodwite" but "men's bloodwite": it is so called because it is paid by men collectively, that is, by the guild as a whole. It is noteworthy that the "guild" (*verv'*) as mentioned in these clauses is a free association of neighbors: not everyone living in a given locality is considered a member of the guild but only those who agree to pay their share in the guild's liabilities.

ARTICLE 13. And for the farm steward or the field overseer, 12 *grivna*.

ARTICLE 14. And for a contract laborer, 5 *grivna*; and as much for a boyar's contract laborer.

Concerning the Handicraftsman or Handicraftswoman

ARTICLE 15. And for the handicraftsman or a handicraftswoman, 12 *grivna*.

ARTICLE 16. And for a peasant or a slave, 5 *grivna*; and for a female slave, 6 *grivna*.

ARTICLE 17. And for the tutor, 12 *grivna*, and the same amount for the nurse, even be he or she a slave.

Concerning the Bloodwite in the Case of a Reported [Homicide]

ARTICLE 18. And if a man [not caught in the very act of committing a murder] is accused of homicide, he has to produce 7 witnesses [to prove his innocence, in order] to reject the bloodwite. And if he is a Varangian or other [alien], then [he needs two witnesses only].

ARTICLE 19. And when bones are found or a [decomposed] corpse, no bloodwite is to be imposed, since they do not know the name [of the dead man] and cannot identify him.

And if [the Defendant] Rejects the Bloodwite

ARTICLE 20. And if [the defendant] rejects the bloodwite [with the aid of witnesses], he has to pay one *grivna* of *kuna* to the clerk for the discontinuance; and the man who brought the accusation pays [to the clerk] another *grivna*; and for [the rejection of] the bloodwite, 9 [*kuna*] as proceedings costs.

ARTICLE 21. And if [the defendant] is unable to produce witnesses but [in his turn] accuses his accuser of the homicide, let them be given an ordeal by iron.

ARTICLE 22. And the same refers to all lawsuits, including theft and other accusations. If the [stolen] thing is not produced, give him [that is, the plaintiff] [ordeal by] iron even against his will [in case the amount of the damages] is over one half of a *grivna* gold. If [the amount] is less [than a half *grivna* gold] but over 2 [silver] *grivna*, [the ordeal is] by water. And if the amount is less [than 2 silver

---

ARTICLE 16. See note to Article 26 (pp. 32, 33).

grivna], then let him [the plaintiff] take the oath concerning his money.

ARTICLE 23. If anyone strikes [another] with a sword without unsheathing it, or with the hilt, a 12 *grivna* fine for the offense.

ARTICLE 24. He who unsheathes his sword but does not strike, one *grivna* of *kuna*.

ARTICLE 25. If anyone hits another with a club or a bowl or a [drinking] horn or the butt [of a tool or a vessel], 12 *grivna*.

ARTICLE 26. If the man [who has been hit], will not endure it and strikes [his offender] with a sword, he is not guilty.

ARTICLE 27. If anyone cuts [another's] arm, and the arm is severed, or shrinks, or if he cuts a leg, or an eye, or the nose, then [he pays] half a bloodwite, 20 *grivna*, and the [injured] man receives 10 *grivna* for his injuries.

ARTICLE 28. If he cuts any of the fingers, a 3 *grivna* fine, and one *grivna* of *kuna* to the injured man.

If a Bloody Man Appears [to Seek Justice]

ARTICLE 29. If a man smeared with blood or blue [from bruises] comes to [the prince's] court, he needs no eyewitness [to prove the offense], and [his assailant] pays a 3 *grivna* fine; if there is no mark [of injury] upon him, he has to produce an eyewitness [to testify] word for word; and the one who started [the fight] pays 60 *kuna*. And if a man comes smeared with blood but it is subsequently proved by witnesses that it was he who started [the fight], then the beating he received serves him as remuneration.

ARTICLE 30. If anyone strikes another with a sword but does not kill him, [he pays] a 3 *grivna* [fine to the prince] and [the expenses] of the treatment of the wound to the [injured man] himself; if he kills [the man he struck, he pays] the bloodwite.

ARTICLE 31. If a man pulls a man toward himself or pushes him, or hits him in the face, or beats him with a rod, two eyewitnesses are to be brought, and the fine is 3 *grivna*; in case he is a Varangian or a Kolbiag, then a full number of eyewitnesses should be brought and an oath is to be taken.

On Slaves

ARTICLE 32. And if a slave should conceal himself, and the owner announces it in the market place, and for three days nobody brings him in, and [the owner] should find him on the third day, he may take his slave and he [who concealed the slave] pays three *grivna* fine.

If Anyone Rides Another's Horse

ARTICLE 33. If anyone rides another's horse without asking [the owner's permission], three *grivna* fine.

ARTICLE 34. If anyone loses his horse, or weapons, or clothes, and announces it in the market place and later recognizes [his lost property] in his own town [at another's house] he takes it back, and [the offender] pays three *grivna* for the offense.

ARTICLE 35. If anyone recognizes [at another's] his property lost or stolen from him, such as a horse, or clothes, or cattle, do not say "It is mine," but: "Let us go for confrontation to the party where you received it" [and] settle it by confrontation. He who is guilty, assumes the responsibility for stealing; [the owner] takes his property; and if anything had been damaged, [the guilty] one must pay for it; and if the guilty one is a horse thief, he shall be surrendered to the prince for banishment; if he is a house thief, he pays three *grivna* [to the prince].

On Confrontment

ARTICLE 36. And if the investigation takes place in the same town, the plaintiff has to go to the last confrontation; if the investigation is transferred to other towns, the plaintiff has to go to the third confrontation only; and the third party pays [the original owner], for what has been found, and with it goes through the last confrontation; and the [original] plaintiff has to wait until the end of the investigation; and when the last [guilty] party is found, he pays the damages as well as the fine.

On Theft

ARTICLE 37. Similarly, if anyone buys stolen goods, be it a horse, or clothes, or cattle, he has to produce two freemen or the toll collector [to certify the fact of his buying it]; if he cannot state from whom he bought [the goods], his eyewitnesses have to swear [that he did buy the goods] and the plaintiff takes his property; and if there are losses, he [the plaintiff] may lament them; and he [who bought the stolen goods] may lament his money, since he does not know from whom he bought [the goods]. And if eventually he should recognize [the man] from whom he bought them, he receives his money from that [man], and the latter pays the damages and a fine to the prince.

If Anyone Finds His [Stolen] Slave

ARTICLE 38. If anyone finds his stolen slave and apprehends him, he must, as in the case of other property litigations, bring him along until the third confrontment; then, he must take [from the third party] some slave instead of his slave and give to him [the third party] his slave as material evidence, and he [the third party] proceeds to the last confrontment. And he [the slave] is not a beast; [in this case] the buyer cannot say, "I do not know from whom I bought him" [because the slave can talk]; and thus by the slave's word one proceeds to the end, and when the final thief is found, [the third party] returns the slave [to the original owner] and takes back his own; and he [the final thief] pays the damages and 12 *grivna* fine to the prince for the stolen slave.

More on Confrontment

ARTICLE 39. And from one's own town to a foreign land there is no confrontment; the intermediary party has to produce, in the usual way, witnesses or the toll collector, in whose presence he bought [the goods]; the plaintiff takes back [such] object [as is available] and may lament the rest which he lost; and [the intermediary party] may lament his money.

On Theft

ARTICLE 40. If they kill any thief near the barn or in any other kind of thievery, they kill him like a dog; but if they hold him until dawn, they have to bring him to the prince's court. If they kill [the thief] and some people had seen him bound, they have to pay 12 *grivna* for the offense.

ARTICLE 41. If anyone steals cattle from the stable or [things from the] barn, if he is alone, he pays 3 *grivna* and 30 *kuna*; if there are many [thieves], each pays 3 *grivna* and 30 *kuna*.

More on Theft

ARTICLE 42. If anyone steals cattle in the field, or sheep, or goats, or pigs, 60 *kuna;* if there are many [thieves], each [pays] 60 *kuna.*

ARTICLE 43. If anyone steals grain from a threshing court or from a pit, irrespective of how many [thieves] there are, each [pays] 3 *grivna* and 30 *kuna.*

ARTICLE 44. And the owner [of the stolen cattle and goods] takes back the object if there is any at hand, and receives half a *grivna* [damage refund] for each year [during which the thieves used it].

ARTICLE 45. And if there be no object at hand, and [the object stolen] was the prince's horse, [the offender] pays 3 *grivna;* and for [the commoner's] horse, 2 *grivna.*

And the Following Are the Amends for [Stolen] Cattle

ARTICLE 45A. For a mare, 7 *kuna;* for an ox, 1 *grivna;* for a cow, 40 *kuna,* for a three year old [cow], 30 *kuna,* for a second year [cow], half a *grivna,* for a heifer, 5 *kuna;* for a sow, 5 *kuna,* and for a sucking pig, 1 *nogata;* for a ewe, 5 *kuna,* for a ram, 1 *nogata;* and for a [young] stallion nobody rode on, 1 *grivna* of *kuna,* [and] for a colt, 6 *nogata;* and for milk, 6 *nogata.* These amends to be paid to the prince by the [free] peasants liable to fines.

And in regard to Slaves Who Be Thieves, the Prince's Ordinance Is as Follows

ARTICLE 46. If slaves, be they the prince's or the boyars', or the monasteries', happen to be thieves, the prince does not fine them since they are not freemen, but they are to pay double for the offense to the plaintiff.

If Anyone Sues [Another] for Money

ARTICLE 47. If anyone sues another for money [loaned] and the latter denies the charges, he has to produce witnesses who must take an oath, and [if they do so], he receives his money back; if the loan has been overdue for many years, [the debtor] has to pay 3 *grivna* for the offense.

ARTICLE 48. If a merchant lends another merchant money for buying [some goods] or for trading, he is not required to do it in the

---

ARTICLE 45A. "For a mare, 7 *kuna.*" The figure is obviously a faulty one; in other manuscripts, "60 *kuna,*" as might have been expected.

presence of witnesses; there is no need of witnesses for him, but he takes the oath himself in case [the one who received the loan] denies the charges.

On Storage

ARTICLE 49. If anyone stores his goods at another's house, there is no need of witnesses; but if he extends claims for a large amount, he who stored the goods has to swear [as follows]: "You stored at my house such and such volume only." Because [he who accepted goods for storage] did a favor to [the owner of the goods] and kept them safe.

On Interest

ARTICLE 50. If anyone lends money at interest, or honey or grain on accruement, he has to produce witnesses; he receives interest or accruement according to the rate agreed upon.

On Monthly Interest

ARTICLE 51. As to the monthly interest, [the lender] shall collect it on short-term [loans] only; if the money has been used for a year, let him [the lender] receive the interest at the third-of-the-year rate, and the monthly rate interest is annulled.

ARTICLE 52. If there were no witnesses, and the amount of money [lent] was not over 3 *grivna*, he has to take an oath; if the amount was greater, they say to him, "It is your fault, you should have done it in the presence of witnesses."

[II. VLADIMIR MONOMACH'S STATUTE]

THE STATUTE OF VLADIMIR, SON OF VSEVOLOD

ARTICLE 53. After the death of [Prince] Sviatopolk, [Prince] Vladimir, son of Vsevolod, called his councilors [for a meeting] at

---

ARTICLE 51. It is plain from this clause that the monthly rate of interest on loans was higher than the third-of-the-year rate. Goetz thinks that *tret'* ("a third") means here "third of the amount lent" ($33\frac{1}{3}$ per cent) and not "third-of-the-year"; his surmise is not acceptable from my point of view.

ARTICLE 53. Prince Vladimir, known as Monomach because of the connection of his family with the Byzantine house of that name, was the son of

Berestov. [The following were present:] Ratibor, the chiliarch of Kiev; Prokopii, the chiliarch of Belgorod; Stanislav, the chiliarch of Pereiaslav; Nazhir; Miroslav; and Ivanko Chudinovich, of

Vsevolod, prince of Kiev from 1078 to 1093 (see note to the preamble to the *Pravda* of Iaroslav's sons in the Short Version, pp. 29, 30). Vsevolod's successor on the throne of Kiev was Sviatopolk, son of Iziaslav. Prince Sviatopolk died in 1113. His death was followed by riots in Kiev which amounted to an abortive social revolution. (See Introduction, Section III, p. 16.) Vladimir's first move was to call a council of state for the discussion and approval of new laws intended to improve the position of the middle and lower classes. Three high dignitaries of the rank of "chiliarch" (*tysiatsky*) were present at the meeting: Ratibor, Prokopii, and Stanislav. In addition, two other of Vladimir's councilors: Nazhir and Miroslav; and Ivanko Chudinovich as a deputy of Prince Oleg, son of Sviatoslav. "Chudinovich" means "son of Chudin." The latter, as we know, had taken part in the meeting of the three elder princes in 1072. Ratibor is mentioned in the Laurentian chronicle as Vladimir's envoy sent to Sviatopolk in 1100. A certain Stanislav is mentioned in the Laurentian chronicle under the year 1136 as a boyar of the Prince of Pereiaslav, but it may have been another man of the same name. A Kiev boyar by the name of Zhiroslav Nazhirovich, that is, son of Nazhir—in all probability, a son of Vladimir's councilor—is mentioned in the Hypatian chronicle under the year 1160. In the same chronicle, under the year 1146, a Kievan boyar by the name of Miroslav is mentioned, presumably the participant of the 1113 conference. Let us now assay the contents of the clause—the first in the series of enactments approved by the conference. Except for Goetz and Dovnar-Zapolsky, all of the commentators understood the clause as an evidence of the fact that three collections of interest at the third-of-the-year rate would considerably surpass the amount loaned. According to Kliuchevsky, the rate must have been 50 per cent, two payments of interest equaling the amount loaned. Goetz, as has already been mentioned (see note to Article 51, above), understood the rate of interest as $33\frac{1}{3}$ per cent, payable at the end of each year. In my opinion Dovnar-Zapolsky was the only scholar who approached the problem with sound judgment since he refused to see in the clause any reference to a specific percentage of interest. Indeed, if we examine the clause in conjunction with Articles 51 and 53A, it is obvious that the intention of the legislator was, in this case, not to limit the rate of the third-of-the-year interest (whatever it may have been), but to make it illegal to collect interest on such a rate for money loaned over a year. In case the loan was not returned within a year, the yearly rate of interest, mentioned in Article 53A, should be automatically applied. The yearly rate was of course lower than the third-of-the-year rate, but we do not know how much lower. If the lender failed to agree to the yearly rate, he forfeited his right to claim his money back, as a penalty for not obeying the law.

[Prince] Oleg's retinue. And they ordered that he who lends money at third-of-the-year rates be limited by the third collection of interest. If he has collected interest for two [third-of-the-year] terms, he receives [also] his money back; but if he has collected interest for three terms, he cannot get his money back.

ARTICLE 53A. If anyone receives yearly interest [at the rate of] 10 *kuna* for 1 *grivna*, this is not annulled.

If a Merchant Be Shipwrecked

ARTICLE 54. If a merchant with another's money in his hands is shipwrecked or loses [his goods] in war or in fire, they should not apply pressure on him, nor sell his entire property, but let him repay [the lender] in yearly installments; because his ruin is from God, and he is not guilty. If he squanders another's goods on drink or [wrecks them] in a brawl, or damages them through his foolishness, then the lenders may choose: if they so wish, they wait for their goods; if not, they sell his entire property.

ARTICLE 53A. This article establishes a ceiling on the yearly rate of interest on loans for the period of one year, or more: 10 *kuna* on each *grivna* loaned. In view of the existence of different systems of monetary units in that period in Russia (see Introduction, Section VII, pp. 23, 24) it is of primary importance to determine, first of all, what is the relation of *kuna* to the *grivna*, and what kind of *grivna* is meant here. Most of the commentators are of the opinion that the *grivna* of *kuna* is meant. Even so, we face another dilemma: while some scholars think that one *grivna* of *kuna* consisted of 50 *kuna*, others try to prove that there were only 25 *kuna* in one *grivna* of *kuna*. In the first case, 10 *kuna* on a *grivna* would represent an interest rate of 20 per cent; in the second case, 40 per cent. This last figure was accepted by Kliuchevsky. However, one may doubt that the *grivna* mentioned in this clause is a *grivna* of *kuna*. In large-scale commercial loans and other transactions of this period the count was almost always in silver. Thus, the *grivna* must mean the silver *grivna*. As we know, one silver *grivna* was equal to four *grivna* of *kuna* (see Introduction, Section VII, p. 24). Thus, for computing the real interest rate we have to divide the above-mentioned alternate figures, 40 per cent and 20 per cent, by four in each case. Accordingly, we may think of an interest rate of either 10 or 5 per cent. It would not be amiss to point out in this connection that in the Byzantine law of the eleventh century the approved rate of interest on loans varied from 5.5 to 8.3 per cent, depending on the terms of the loan (Zachariä von Lingenthal, *Geschichte des griechisch-römischen Rechts*, 3d ed., Berlin, 1892, p. 311).

On Debts

ARTICLE 55. If anyone is indebted to many creditors and there comes a merchant from another town, or a foreigner, and without knowing [of the man's indebtedness] lends him goods, and he would not pay him and [when the last lender would claim his money back] the former lenders object to his being satisfied first, they [all the lenders] shall bring the man to the market place and sell his entire property. From the proceeds, they first repay the [out of town or foreign] merchant, and the balance is divided among his home-town creditors. If the prince's money was involved, they first pay the prince, and the balance is divided among the others. And he who had [already] collected much interest, [now] receives nothing.

If an Indentured Laborer Runs Away

ARTICLE 56. If an indentured laborer runs away from his lord, he becomes the latter's slave. But if he departs openly, to sue for his money [and goes] to the prince, or to the judges, to complain of the injustice on the part of his lord, they do not reduce him to slavery but give him justice.

More on the Indentured Laborer

ARTICLE 57. If an agricultural indentured laborer ruins a war horse, he does not pay for it. But if the lord from whom he received money intrusts to him [a work horse to work with] plow and harrow and he ruins it, he has to pay for it. But if the lord sends him away for some business of his [that is, the lord's] and [the work horse] perishes, he [the laborer] need not pay for it.

ARTICLE 56. "Indentured laborer," *zakup*. *Zakup* was a laborer who received his seasonal or yearly wages in advance; or who borrowed money from the lord and had to work to repay both the loan and the interest. "To sue for his money," *iskati kun*. Grekov interprets this phrase in the sense "to look for money," that is, to try to obtain from somebody funds to repay the loan to the lord in order to cover the indenture.

ARTICLE 57. "Agricultural indentured laborer," *roleinyi zakup*, from *rolia*, "plow land." "War horse," *voisky kon'*. In some later copies, *svoisky kon'*, "his own horse." *Voisky* is apparently the correct reading. Presumably, the lord was supposed to have special grooms—his slaves—to care for the steeds. A war horse cost more that any indentured laborer could be expected to pay.

More on the Indentured Laborer

ARTICLE 58. If they steal [cattle] from [the lord's] stable, the laborer does not have to pay for it. But if [the laborer] loses cattle on the field because he failed to drive them to the yard and did not lock them where the lord ordered him, or because he worked for himself and neglected working for the lord, then he has to pay.

ARTICLE 59. If the lord offends the indentured laborer and seizes his money or his movables, he has to return all this and pay 60 *kuna* for the offense.

ARTICLE 60. If the lord transfers the indenture on the laborer [to a third person] for money, [the transaction is annulled:] the [first] lord has to return the money he accepted and pay 3 *grivna* fine.

ARTICLE 61. If the lord sells the indentured laborer into slavery, the laborer is free from all obligations for the money [he had received from the lord], and the lord pays a 12 *grivna* fine for the offense.

ARTICLE 62. If the lord beats the indentured laborer for good reason, he is without fault; but if he beats the indentured laborer foolishly, being drunk, and without any fault on the part of the indentured laborer, he has to pay for the offense to the indentured laborer the same fine as it would be for a freeman.

On Slaves

ARTICLE 63. If a full slave steals another's horse, [the owner of the slave] has to pay 2 *grivna*.

ARTICLE 64. If an indentured laborer steals [a horse] or some other [beast], his lord is responsible for him. And when they find him, the lord first pays for the horse or anything else he stole, and then [the indentured laborer] is his full slave. And if the lord does not want to pay in behalf of [his indentured laborer], he sells him, and first reimburses [the owner] for the horse, or the ox, or cattle, whatever was stolen, and keeps the balance.

And if a Slave Strikes [a Freeman]

ARTICLE 65. And if a slave strikes a freeman and hides in the

---

ARTICLE 65. This clause, although inserted by the editors of the Expanded Version among the sections of Vladimir Monomach's Statute, obviously does not belong in it. Compare Article 17, p. 29.

house, and his lord will not surrender him, the lord pays for him a 12 *grivna* [fine]; and then whenever and wherever the injured man meets the offender, who struck him, [Prince] Iaroslav ordered to [allow him] to kill the offender, but his sons, after their father's death, ordered the matter to be settled with the alternative of payment: either to bind the slave [to a post] and beat him, or to accept 1 *grivna* for the offense to his honor.

On Witnesses

ARTICLE 66. And the slave cannot serve as a witness; however, at need, when there is no freeman, a boyar's steward [even if he is a slave] may be a witness, but no other [slave]. And in a minor litigation, at need, an indentured laborer may serve as witness.

[III. OTHER ENACTMENTS]

On Beards

ARTICLE 67. If anyone tears [another's] beard, and [the offended either comes to the court] with the sign of it, or produces men [as witnesses], [the offender pays] a 12 *grivna* fine; but if there is a claim and no men [to support it], there is no fine.

On Teeth

ARTICLE 68. If they knock out anyone's tooth, and blood is visible in his mouth, or men [as witnesses] are produced, 12 *grivna* fine, and 1 *grivna* [damages] for the tooth.

[On Theft of Game]

ARTICLE 69. If anyone steals a beaver, 12 *grivna*.

ARTICLE 70. If there are traces on the ground or any evidence of hunting, or a net, the guild must search for the poacher or pay the fine.

If Anyone Obliterates the Sign on a Beehive [or Any Other Marker]

ARTICLE 71. If anyone obliterates the sign on a beehive, 12 *grivna*.

ARTICLE 72. If anyone cuts an apiary boundary [hedge], or plows through a field boundary, or bars [another's] yard boundary by paling, 12 *grivna* fine.

ARTICLE 73. If anyone cuts a landmark oak, 12 *grivna* fine.

And the Following Is the Supply Quota

ARTICLE 74. And this is the supply quota: [to the collector of fines], 12 *grivna*; to the clerk, 2 *grivna* and 20 *kuna*; and he himself and the clerk are to ride on two horses to be given oats; and as to meat, they give them a sheep or a portion of beef; and other food as much as their stomachs will hold; to the scribe, 10 *kuna*; loading [fee] 5 *kuna*; fur [fee], 2 *nogata*.

And the Following Is on Beehives

ARTICLE 75. If anyone cuts a beehive [from a tree], 3 *grivna* fine; and for the tree [on which the beehive is placed], half a *grivna*.

ARTICLE 76. If anyone carries the bees away, 3 *grivna* fine; and for honey, in case it had not been already cut out, 10 *kuna*. For [damaging] a honeyless beehive, 5 *kuna*.

ARTICLE 77. If the thief is not on hand, they pursue him on his trail. If the trail leads to a village or to a camp and they [the villagers] cannot prove that it passes [the village]; or if they would not follow the trail, or would evade it, they have to pay the damages as well as the fine. And they have to follow the trail with outside people and witnesses present. If they lose the trail on a highway, with no village in sight, or in a wilderness where there is no village nor people, they do not have to pay the fine, nor the damages.

On Peasants

ARTICLE 78. If a peasant inflicts pain on another peasant without the prince's authorization, 3 *grivna* fine, and 1 *grivna* of *kuna* [amends] for the pain. If he inflicts pain on the prince's bailiff, 12 *grivna* fine, and 1 *grivna* [amends] for the pain.

ARTICLE 79. If anyone steals a boat, 60 *kuna* fine, and the boat to be returned in kind. For a seagoing boat, 3 *grivna*; for a decked boat, 2 *grivna*; for a canoe, 20 *kuna*; for a barge, 1 *grivna*.

On Hunting Nets

ARTICLE 80. If anyone cuts a rope in the hunting net, 3 *grivna* fine, and to the owner 1 *grivna* of *kuna* [damages] for the rope.

ARTICLE 81. If anyone steals from a hunting net a hawk or a falcon, 3 *grivna* fine, and to the owner, 1 *grivna;* and for a dove, 9 *kuna;* for a fowl, 9 *kuna;* for a duck, 30 *kuna;* for a goose, 30 *kuna;* for a swan, 30 *kuna;* and for a crane, 30 *kuna*.

[On Stealing Hay]

ARTICLE 82. And for [stealing] hay or lumber, 9 *kuna* [fine], and to the owner according to the number of cartloads stolen, 2 *nogata* for a cartload.

On the Threshing Court

ARTICLE 83. If anyone sets fire to a threshing court, he is to be banished and his house confiscated; first, the damages are paid, and the prince takes care of the rest. The same for setting fire to anyone's homestead.

ARTICLE 84. And whoever vilely maims or slaughters [another's] horse or cattle [shall pay] 12 *grivna* fine, and, for the damages, amends to the owner.

ARTICLE 85. In all the above litigations the trial is with freemen as witnesses. If the witness is a slave, he is not to take [a direct] part in the trial; but if the plaintiff so desires, he seizes [the defendant] and says as follows: "I am seizing thee on the ground of this [man's] words, but it is I who seize thee, and not the slave." And he takes him [the defendant] to the ordeal. If he [the plaintiff] succeeds in proving his guilt, he takes back from him [the defendant] his own; if he does not succeed in accusing him, he pays him 1 *grivna* [amends] for the pain inflicted, since he seized him on the ground of a slave's words.

ARTICLE 86. And they have to pay 40 *kuna* ordeal-by-iron fee; and to the sheriff, 5 *kuna;* and to the clerk, half a *grivna*. Those are the ordeal-by-iron payments,—who receives what.

ARTICLE 87. If [the plaintiff] seizes [the defendant] for the ordeal by iron on the ground of a freeman's word; or if there is a [definite] suspicion [against the defendant]; or if [the witnesses saw the defendant] pass at night near [the spot where the crime was committed]; or [in the case of the defendant's acquittal] if perchance he is not burned [at the ordeal], he who seized him need not pay [amends] for the pain inflicted, but only the ordeal-by-iron fee.

On Women

ARTICLE 88. If anyone kills a woman he is tried in the same way as if he killed a man. If he is found guilty [he shall pay] one half of the bloodwite, 20 *grivna*.

ARTICLE 89. And there is no bloodwite for either a male or a female slave; but if a slave is killed without any fault of his, [the killer] has to pay amends for the male, as well as for the female, slave; and to the prince, 12 *grivna* fine.

If a Peasant Dies

ARTICLE 90. If a peasant dies [without male descendants] his estate goes to the prince; if there are daughters left in the house, each receives a portion [of the estate]; if they are married, they receive no portion.

On the Estates of Boyars and Members of the Princely Retinue

ARTICLE 91. In regard to the boyars and the members of the princely retinue, the estate does not go to the prince, but, if there are no sons left, the daughters inherit.

ARTICLE 92. If anyone, before dying, makes a settlement dividing his estate between his children, his will stands. If he dies without a will, the estate is divided between his children [in equal shares], except for a portion which goes [to a monastery] for prayers for the soul [of the deceased].

ARTICLE 93. If the wife survives her husband, she receives a portion [of the estate in usufruct]; and whatever her husband had given her [by a special settlement], she owns that, but she does not inherit the estate.

ARTICLE 94. [In case the deceased had been married more than once], if there are children left, those by the first wife inherit their mother's share; and whatever the deceased gave to her the children inherit from their mother's estate.

ARTICLE 95. If there is [an unmarried] sister in the house, she has no share in the estate, but her brothers marry her [off] with such dowry as they can.

The Following Is in Regard to Building Town [Walls]

ARTICLE 96. And these are the payments to the town builder: at his starting a section of the town [wall] he receives 1 *kuna*; and at completing it, 1 *nogata*; and for food and drink and for meat and for fish, 7 *kuna* a week; 7 loaves of bread; 7 measures of millet; and 7 buckets of oats for 4 horses. He continues to receive all this until he completes the wall; but as to malt, they give him 10 buckets once only.

On Bridgebuilders

ARTICLE 97. And those are the payments to the bridgebuilder. When he completes the bridge, he receives 1 *nogata* for each 10 ells. If he repairs an old bridge, irrespective of how many sections of the bridge he may have repaired, he receives 1 *kuna* for each section. And the bridgebuilder and his assistant keep two horses to be provided with 4 buckets of oats a week; and [the bridgebuilder and his assistant receive] such food as they can eat.

The Following Is on the Estate of One Deceased

ARTICLE 98. If there are children by a man's female slave left, they do not inherit and are to be set free after his death.

ARTICLE 99. If there are small children left in the house who are not able to take care of themselves, and their mother should marry, he who is their nearest relative assumes care of them as well as of all their property and the house until they be of age; and the property is to be given to him [in trust] in the presence of men. And if he succeeds in making a profit on that property, he keeps it; that is, he returns to the children the original amount, and keeps all the profit, since it was he who fed them and took care of them. Similarly in regard to the progeny of both the slaves and cattle; everything should be accounted for; if [the trustee] loses anything, he has to make amends to the children. If it is the stepfather who takes care of the children and their estate the settlement is identical.

ARTICLE 100. And the father's homestead is not subject to any division of the estate, but [is given] to the youngest son.

On the Wife Who Agrees to Manage Her Deceased Husband's Estate

ARTICLE 101. If the wife agrees to manage her deceased husband's estate and then loses the property and marries, she has to pay the children for everything.

ARTICLE 102. If the children do not want to stay on the homestead and she wants to, her will prevails and not the children's; and she remains on the homestead with what her husband had given her, or the portion [of the estate] she received [in usufruct].

ARTICLE 103. And the children cannot dispose of their mother's portion: to whom the mother gives it, he receives it; if she gives it to all of them, they divide it among themselves. If she dies without a will, he in whose home she lived and who fed her, receives her estate.

ARTICLE 104. If there are children left of the same mother by her two [successive] husbands, the children of each respective father receive his estate.

ARTICLE 105. If a stepfather spends some property of the father of his stepson [which he holds in trust] and dies, his son must return to his [half]-brother that which his father spent out of his stepfather's estate, as testified by neighbors; and he keeps what had belonged to his father.

ARTICLE 106. And as to the mother, she may give her portion to that one of her sons, whether by her first or by her second husband, who is kind to her. If all her sons are wicked, she may give her portion to her daughter who feeds her.

The Following Are the Court Fees

ARTICLE 107. And these are the court fees: from each bloodwite [the court fee is] 9 *kuna*, and the constable's fee is 9 *veksha*. And from [litigations about] the beehive lots [the court fee is] 30 *kuna*. And from all other kinds of litigation, the litigant who wins the lawsuit pays [the court fee of] 4 *kuna*, and the constable's fee, 6 *veksha*.

On the Estate of the Deceased

ARTICLE 108. If brothers contend in the prince's court concerning [their father's] estate, the clerk who divides the estate for them receives 1 *grivna* of *kuna*.

On the Fees for Administering an Oath

ARTICLE 109. And these are the oath fees: in homicide cases, 30 *kuna*; in [litigations concerning] the beehive lots, 30 *kuna* minus 3 *kuna*; the same [in litigations concerning] arable land; and at freeing a slave, 9 *kuna*.

On Slavery

ARTICLE 110. Full slavery is of three kinds: [first] if anyone buys [a man] willing [to sell himself into slavery], for not less than half a *grivna*, and produces witnesses and pays [the fee of] 1 *nogata* in the presence of the slave himself. And the second kind of slavery is this: if anyone marries a female slave without special agreement [with her lord]; if he marries her with a special agreement, what he agreed to, stands. And this is the third kind of slavery: if anyone becomes [another's] steward or housekeeper without a special agreement; if there has been an agreement, what has been agreed upon, stands.

ARTICLE 111. And the recipient of a [money] grant is not a slave. And one cannot make a man one's slave because [he received] a grant-in-aid in grain, or [failed to furnish] additional grain [when repaying the grant]; if he fails to complete the term of work [for the grant], he has to return the grant; if he completes the term, he stands cleared.

ARTICLE 110. In the first part of this clause, the case of a man voluntarily selling himself into slavery is assayed, and a minimum price is set for such transactions. "For not less than half a *grivna*," *do polugrivny*. *Do* may mean "up to" or "down to." Here we must interpret it as "down to," that is "not less than half a *grivna*," by analogy with Article 22 where the same expression is used and where it is perfectly clear from the context that "not less than half a *grivna*" is meant. Thus, the object of this clause is to make the procedure of enslavement more difficult and to prevent any possible abuses. If the requirements of the clause be not fulfilled, the transaction is invalid, and the money given by the lord to the applicant is considered not the price paid for the slave but merely a grant. Such grants are dealt with in Article 111.

ARTICLE 111. Grant, *dacha*. Recipient of the grant, *vdach*. The meaning of this section may be better understood through comparison with Article 77 of the *Zakon Sudny Liudem* (see Saturnik, p. 164). The latter reads as follows: "If in the time of a famine a man or a woman gives himself (her-

ARTICLE 112. If a slave runs away and his owner makes due announcement, and someone else, having heard the announcement or knowing about it and understanding that the man is a fugitive slave, gives him some bread or shows him the way [to escape], he has to pay for the male slave 5 *grivna* and for the female slave 6 *grivna*.

ARTICLE 113. If anyone apprehends another's slave and informs the owner, he receives 1 *grivna* for the arrest [of the slave]; if he lets him escape, he has to pay 4 *grivna* but keeps the fifth *grivna* [as his remuneration for the attempted] arrest; in case of a female slave, [he pays] 5 *grivna* and [keeps] the sixth *grivna* for the [attempted] arrest.

ARTICLE 114. If anyone finds by himself his runaway slave in some town the mayor of which did not know about [that slave], he informs the mayor, and the latter sends a clerk with him, and they go and bind the slave, and he gives the clerk 10 *kuna* binding fee, but no remuneration for the arrest. If the slave escapes when he drives him home, that is his loss, nobody has to pay him, since the slave had not been arrested [by any authority, but on the owner's initiative].

ARTICLE 115. If anyone meets another man's slave, not knowing that he is such, and gives him information [about traveling], or keeps him in his own house, and then [that slave] leaves him, he has to swear that he did not know that that man was another's slave, and he is not required to pay [the owner].

ARTICLE 116. If a slave should receive [from anyone] money under false pretense, and the creditor lent it not knowing [that the man was a slave], the owner [of the slave] has to redeem or lose him. If the creditor lent the money knowing [that the man was a slave] he loses his money.

ARTICLE 117. If anyone authorizes his slave to trade and the latter should fall in debt, the owner redeems him but does not lose him.

ARTICLE 118. If anyone buys another man's slave without knowing it, the original owner takes the slave and the buyer receives his money back after swearing that he had bought him without knowing [who he was].

---

self), into [the service of] a lord, he (she) is not a slave; if he (she) leaves the lord, he (she) has to pay 3 *grivna*, but cannot claim any compensation for his (her) work "

ARTICLE 119. [If a runaway slave obtains goods on credit,] the owner takes back the slave, [and assumes his debt], and also takes the goods.

ARTICLE 120. If [a slave] runs away and takes any neighbor's property or goods, his owner pays the damages.

ARTICLE 121. If a slave robs a man, the owner may redeem or surrender him, as well as those who participated with him in the robbery, but not [the slave's] wife and children unless they helped him to rob, or hid [the stolen goods]; in such a case he [the owner of the slave] surrenders them, or else he redeems them all. If freemen participated in the robbery, they are liable for the payment of the fine to the prince.

ARTICLE 119. The text of this article in the Trinity copy is incomplete; in the translation, the initial phrase in brackets has been supplied from another copy. See Goetz, *Das russische Recht*, I, p. 62.

THE CHARTER OF DVINA LAND

[PREAMBLE]. I, the Grand Duke Vasili Dmitrievich of all Russia, have privileged my Dvina boyars as well as the hundreder and my lower-class men of the Dvina Land. Any of my [Moscow] boyars whom I favor by sending as my lieutenant to the Dvina Land, or any of the Dvina boyars I favor with lieutenancy, shall rule in accordance with this my grand-ducal charter.

ARTICLE 1. And if there occurs a crime subject to bloodwite, the [Dvina] people have to search for the murderer; and if they fail to find the murderer, they have to pay to my lieutenants, [for murder], ten rubles; and for a bloody wound, 30 *bela;* and for bruises, 15 *bela;* and the bot, accordingly.

Note. Vladimirsky-Budanov's edition has been used for this translation. The division into articles is likewise Vladimirsky-Budanov's, except that I have subdivided his Article 10 into Articles 10 and 10A.

PREAMBLE. Vasili I, son of Dmitri Donskoy, reigned in Moscow from 1389 to 1425. "Dmitrievich" means "son of Dmitri." I translate the title *Veliky Kniaz* (literally, "Grand Prince") as "Grand Duke" according to the established usage. Note the claim of the Moscow Grand Dukes on the control of "all Russia" in the title. "Dvina" is the Northern Dvina River. On the historical background and the immediate reasons for the issuing of this charter by Grand Duke Vasili, see Introduction, Section VI (pp. 20, 21). "Hundreder," *sotnik;* "lower-class men," *chernye liudi,* literally, "black men." The *chernye liudi* were usually organized in "hundreds," each hundred controlled by a "hundreder." In the Dvina Land, however, as may be seen from this Preamble, there was only one hundreder to supervise the lower-class men in all of the towns. "Lieutenant," *namestnik.*

ARTICLE 1. It is obvious that this clause derives from Articles 3-8 of the Expanded Version of the *Pravda Russkaia* dealing with the collective payment of the bloodwite (*dikaia vira*). *Bela* (or *belka*), in Old Russian, was used in two senses: (1) silver coin (see Introduction, Section VII, p. 24); (2) fur, presumably ermine. In modern Russian, *belka* means "squirrel." In the sixteenth century 100 *bela* equaled one ruble. It seems that at the time of the promulgation of the Dvina charter people in the Dvina region actually used furs for payments.

ARTICLE 2. And if anyone uses insulting language against a boyar, or wounds a boyar, or [beats him so that] he has bruises about him, my lieutenants shall adjudge payments [by the offender] to satisfy the offense to the boyar; and to the knight, accordingly.

ARTICLE 3. And if a fight occurs at a banquet, and the participants settle the mutual offenses before leaving the banquet hall, no fine is collected by either the lieutenants or their squires; but if they settle outside of the banquet hall, each has to pay one marten worth of wool to the lieutenant.

ARTICLE 4. And if anyone plows his neighbor's land-boundary within the village, the fine is one ram; and for plowing a boundary between two villages, 30 *bela*; and for plowing a boundary of the prince's demesne, 120 *bela*; and there is no imprisonment for that.

ARTICLE 5. And if anyone finds an object stolen from him at another's house, the holder of the object shall go to the investigation by confrontment, up to the tenth confrontment, or up to the detection of the thief [if the thief be detected before the tenth confrontment]; and there are no tolls to either the lieutenants or their squires. And the thief shall be fined in proportion to the value of the object, if it is his first theft; if he is detected for the second time, his whole property shall be confiscated; and if detected for the third time, he shall be hanged.

ARTICLE 6. And for settling privately with the criminal, the fine is four rubles. And this is what is meant here: when anyone catches a thief and lets him go for a bribe, and the lieutenant should be informed about it; such is settling with the criminal privately, and nothing else is meant here.

ARTICLE 2. "Knight," *sluga*, literally, servitor. The term *sluga*, was used in this period to denote a prince's councilor of the second rank, lower than a boyar.

ARTICLE 3. "Squire," *dvorianin*. In modern Russian *dvorianin* means "a nobleman." In the fourteenth and fifteenth centuries the term denoted a noble official of a minor rank, lower than *sluga*.

ARTICLE 5. Hanging of the thief for his third theft should be noted as an innovation in regard to the Russian Law: the latter knows no capital punishment. See Introduction, Section II, p. 12.

ARTICLE 6. "Settling with the criminal privately," *samosud*, literally "self-justice," or "taking the law in one's own hands." Only a specific case of *samosud* is dealt with here.

ARTICLE 7. And if anyone loses a [civil] lawsuit for the amount of one ruble, the fee to the lieutenants is half a ruble; and more, or less, proportionally.

ARTICLE 8. And the squire receives for serving the summons in the town of Orlets, 1 *bela*; and if he has to travel to other towns, his allowance for travel expenses is as follows: From Orlets to Matigory, 2 *bela*; to Kolmogory, 2 *bela*; to Kurostrov, 2 *bela*; to Chiukhchelem, 2 *bela*; to Ukhtostrov, 2 *bela*; to Kurgia, 2 *bela*; to Kniazh Ostrov, 4 *bela*; to Lisich Ostrov, 7 *bela*, and to Konechnye Dvory, 10 *bela*; to Nonaksa, 20 *bela*; to Una, 30 *bela*. And from Orlets up the Dvina River, to Krivoe, 1 *bela*; to Rakula, 2 *bela*; to Navolok, 3 *bela*; to Chelmakhta, 4 *bela*; to Emtsa, 5 *bela*; to Kaleia, 10 *bela*; to Kiriegory, 17 *bela*; to Nizhniaia Toima, 30 *bela*. And for administering an oath, double allowance. And the fee for shackling [a suspected criminal], 4 *bela*; but they shackle a man only if there is nobody to vouch for him; and the squire shall not collect anything above [the established service charge]; and if there is a bail, he shall not shackle the man. And the squire shall not accept bribes; and if a bribe is promised, such promise is invalid.

ARTICLE 9. If anyone sues another man, and the squire and the constable summon the defendant and he fails to appear in court, the lieutenants issue a writ against him. And in case the defendant is not a Dvina man, he may produce a bail.

ARTICLE 10. And the fee of the lieutenants for sealing a document is 3 *bela*; and of the secretary, for writing a copy of the court decision, 2 *bela*.

ARTICLE 10A. And the tax to the hundreder and the constable is a bag of rye from each merchant's boat.

ARTICLE 11. And if a lord beats his male or female slave, not intending to kill him or her, and he or she dies, the lord is not subject to trial by the lieutenants, nor is any fine collected.

ARTICLE 12. And my grand-ducal constables shall not enter the Dvina Land, my lieutenants taking care of the administration [of the said Land].

ARTICLE 13. And if [a lieutenant of mine] taxes people exces-

---

ARTICLE 9. "Constable," *podvoisky*, a local official. See note to Article 12, below.

ARTICLE 12. "Constable," *pristav*. This is a Moscow official.

sively, and the people complain to me, I, the Grand Duke, shall order him to appear before me within a term; and if he fails to appear, I shall issue a writ against him, and my constable will collect damages from him.

ARTICLE 14. And the Dvina merchants may carry their goods in boats, or in wagons; and the carriage toll to the lieutenants is, in Ustiug, two bags of salt from each boatload, and two *bela* from each wagonload. And neither the lieutenant, nor the toll officials shall collect from the Dvina merchants anything above that rate. And in Vologda the merchants shall pay two bags of salt from each boatload, and one *bela* from each wagonload; and above that nothing is collected from them, and they may proceed, be it in boats or in wagons, and neither my Ustiug nor my Vologda lieutenants may stop them.

ARTICLE 15. And the traveling merchants may not be tried [by local judges] nor asked to produce a bail in Ustiug, or in Vologda, or in Kostroma; but if there occurs a theft and the stolen object is found [in possession of a traveling merchant], the merchant is to be brought, together with the incriminating evidence, to me, the Grand Duke, and I, the Grand Duke, myself will try him. And [if a traveling merchant is a defendant] in a civil lawsuit, the plaintiff has to make an agreement with him [concerning the time of their appearing before the court] in the presence of my Dvina lieutenants, and the latter will try the case in Dvina Land.

ARTICLE 16. And wherever within my realm the Dvina merchants travel they are not liable to *tamga,* or to *myt,* or to *kostki,* or to storage duties, or to the inspection duties, or to any other custom duties. And whoever offends them contrary to this charter of mine, or whoever does not fulfill the provisions of this charter, will be punished by me, the Grand Duke.

ARTICLE 16. *Tamga* is an internal tax on goods shipped from one locality to another; it was introduced by the Mongols. *Myt* refers to customs duties on goods imported from outside. *Kostki* is obviously another kind of tax or customs duty, but its precise meaning has not been determined.

THE CHARTER OF THE CITY OF PSKOV

[PREAMBLE]. This charter is based on Grand Duke Alexander's charter, and on Prince Constantine's charter, and on records of Pskov's old customs. [It is issued] with the blessing of the fathers—the priests of all the five cathedrals, and of hieromonks, and the deacons, and the priests and all God's clergy—[as approved] by the whole of Pskov, at the city assembly, in the year 6905 [A.M.].

ARTICLE 1. These are the cases subject to trial in the princely

---

Note. Vladimirsky-Budanov's edition has been used for this translation. The division into articles is Vladimirsky-Budanov's except that his articles 75 and 103 have been subdivided each into Articles 75 and 75A, 103 and 103A, respectively.

PREAMBLE. Grand Duke Alexander—presumably Alexander of Tver who reigned in Pskov twice, from 1327 to 1330 and from 1332 to 1337. Constantine, brother of Grand Duke Vasili of Moscow (the grantor of the Dvina Charter), reigned in Pskov thrice in the period between 1407 and 1414. The term "cathedral," *sobor*, had, in Pskov church history, the connotation of "ecclesiastical district." To each such district about one hundred priests were allocated. With the building of new churches and the growth of the clergy, new "cathedrals" were organized. Each group centered around its cathedral church. The oldest of these was the Holy Trinity Cathedral in the Pskov Kremlin. Since five cathedrals are mentioned in the preamble it would not be amiss to point out here that the fifth cathedral district in Pskov was organized in 1462, and the sixth in 1471. On the other hand, the charter is dated in the year 6905 Anno Mundi (according to the Byzantine and Old Russian practice) which corresponds to A.D. 1397. Presumably the charter had been originally issued in 1397 on the basis of Grand Duke Alexander's charter and of the Pskov customary law; later, material from Prince Constantine's charter was added, and some time between 1462 and 1471 (in which period there existed five cathedrals) the charter was revised, but the original date was left intact in the copy. Because the charter was based on several sources and was compiled in several installments, some of the clauses found in the first part are later repeated with but slight variations. The most likely date of the final approval of the charter is 1467, since in this year the Moscow grand duke sent to Pskov Prince F. Iu. Shuisky as his lieutenant.

court: if they rob a locked barn; or a sledge covered by a rug; or a packed wagon; or a decked boat; or if they steal cattle; or [grain] from a pit; or hay from a haystack—all that is subject to the princely court: 9 *denga* fine. And in a highway robbery, raid, burglary, the fine is 9 *grivna;* and [fees] 19 *denga* to the prince, and 4 *denga* to the mayor.

ARTICLE 2. And the archbishop's lieutenant holds his court; and neither the prince nor his judges shall interfere with it. And the [archbishop's] lieutenants shall not interfere with the princely court.

ARTICLE 3. And when a mayor is installed in his office, he shall swear that he will conduct the trials justly, in accordance with his oath; and will not embezzle municipal funds; and will not avenge through his court decisions; and will not favor his relatives; and will ruin no innocent, nor help a culprit. And no man shall be punished either by the court or by the city assembly without due examination.

ARTICLE 4. And the prince and the mayor shall not conduct trials at the city assembly; they shall conduct the trials in the prince's palace, consulting the law, according to their oath; and if they do not conduct trials in accordance with the law, God will be their judge at Christ's second advent. And neither the prince nor the mayor shall ever accept bribes.

ARTICLE 5. And when a prince's man proceeds as [prince's] lieutenant to a borough, he must swear that he will be loyal to Pskov and will conduct trials justly in accordance with his oath. And if he has to go to some . . .

ARTICLE 6. And when a mayor completes the term of his office he must have all lawsuits and trials brought to conclusion; and his successor shall not reopen those cases.

According to the chronicles, Shuisky "kissed the cross," promising to preserve "all Pskov customs" intact. For "city assembly," *veche,* see Introduction, Sections IV and V, pp. 18–20.

According to Cherepnin and Iakovlev, the following articles belong to Grand Duke Alexander's charter: 1, 7–13, 20–27, 34–37, 46–50. This seems plausible enough. As to Prince Constantine's charter, the same scholars consider Articles 52–71 its traces; according to Engelman, however, Constantine's charter would begin with Article 77 and run to Article 108. Other students of the Pskov law offer still different suggestions.

ARTICLE 5. Left unfinished in the manuscript. "Borough," *prigorod,* see Introduction, Section IV, p. 18.

CHARTER OF PSKOV

ARTICLE 7. And life is denied to one who commits theft in the Kremlin; and to the horse stealer; and to the spy; and to the incendiary.

ARTICLE 8. If anyone commits a theft in the city and is detected, they, as a favor, fine him for his first theft, and for the second; if he is detected for the third time, life is denied to him. [But the above favor] does not apply to the Kremlin thief.

ARTICLE 9. And if there is litigation concerning land or water, and there is a homestead on that plot of land or there are tilled fields on it, and [the defendant] has toiled on and possessed that land, or water, for four or five years, that defendant must refer to his neighbors, four or five of them. And if the neighbors referred to appear before the court and state justly as if facing God, that the defendant is right and that he has toiled on and possessed that land, or water, for four or five years and that during this time the plaintiff never sued him for that land or water, nor used it, then his [defendant's] land or water, is free from any claims; and he must not take the oath. And [the plaintiff] who did not sue for nor use [that land or water] during that time, has lost his lawsuit.

ARTICLE 10. And when there is litigation about woodland let the two parties produce their deeds on land, and if the deeds overlap, the two claimants shall call land surveyors and the boundaries shall be examined in respect to both deeds; and the land surveyors shall state the case before the supreme court; and if the claims cannot be settled by land surveying, the court orders a duel.

ARTICLE 7. This clause establishes capital punishment for four categories of criminals. The first is that of the *krimskoy tat'*, which is obviously a misspelling for *kromskoy tat'*, a "Kremlin thief," that is, one who commits theft in the precincts of the Pskov Kremlin (*Krom*). The reason for the heavier punishment of a "Kremlin thief" than an ordinary thief is the special importance of the Kremlin both as a citadel and as a religious center (the site of the Holy Trinity Cathedral); also as a storage place for supplies and provisions of different kinds belonging both to the city and to wealthy burghers. It may be added that the manuscript contains a marginal note to this article, correcting *krimskoy tat'* to *khramskoy tat'* (church treasury thief). In Article 9 of the Code of Laws (*Sudebnik*) of Grand Duke Ivan III (1497)—which is based upon this clause of the Pskov charter—we read *tserkovny tat'* (church thief).

ARTICLE 10. "Supreme Court," *gospoda*, literally, "the Lords." "Duel," *pole*, literally "field," that is, the duel field (*campus* in Frankish legislation). See Introduction, Section II (p. 12).

ARTICLE 11. And that one of the litigants who wins. . . .

ARTICLE 12. And that one of the litigants [who is defeated] stands accused and his deeds are annulled; and the winner receives the land and the copy of the court decision. And the prince and the mayor and the hundreders, all of them together, collect the court fees, 10 *denga*.

ARTICLE 13. And if anyone wants to redeem land now held by another [according to the provisions of the original deed], and the man from whom they want to take the land has deeds old [enough to prove that the term, during which the claimant had the right to redeem the land, has expired], it is left to that man's will: either to go to the duel or to let the plaintiff swear that the redemption clause on the original deed is still valid.

ARTICLE 14. [If a man dies] and another produces a [noncertified] note to claim his goods that were allegedly accepted for storage by the deceased, and sues the executors for the goods stored, be it silver, or clothes, or jewels, or any other chattels, and [it happens that the deceased] has left a written will duly recorded in the files [at the Holy Trinity Cathedral], no claim against the executors is valid unless the plaintiff produces a written agreement or a pledge. And if there is a pledge or a written agreement, the plaintiff may start a lawsuit. And, vice versa, if the executors hold neither a pledge nor a copy of the written agreement [given to the deceased by the man they intend to sue] they may not sue him for a loan, or for shares in trade, or for storage, or for anything of the kind.

ARTICLE 15. And if anyone dies [without a will], and his father, or mother, or son, or brother, or sister, or some other relative is left, they are entitled to sue each other, but not the outsiders, both for property given by the deceased to some of them and for property taken from the deceased by some of them, even if they do not have a pledge or a written agreement.

ARTICLE 11. Unfinished in the manuscript.

ARTICLE 13. In order properly to understand this clause one has to take into consideration the peculiarity of the juridical nature of the sale contract in the medieval Russian law. It was always assumed that the seller retained the right of redeeming the property he sold, in any case within a term agreed upon.

ARTICLE 14. A "non-certified note," *doska*, "board," "table" (originally, a tally; a writing tablet). Certified notes and agreements were recorded in the archives office at the Holy Trinity Cathedral, and a copy of each filed there.

CHARTER OF PSKOV 65

ARTICLE 16. And if anyone because of some emergency, such as a fire or being for his sins threatened by people in the time of an uprising, hands to another man goods or anything else for storage, and the man [to whom he trusted his goods] denies that he accepted anything, the plaintiff has to produce. . . .

ARTICLE 17. And if anyone, having come from a foreign land, or because of a fire, or in the time of an uprising, [hands another goods for storage and then claims them back] within a week, and the man [to whom he entrusted the goods] denies [that he accepted anything], the court leaves the procedure to the defendant's will: if he wants it, he takes the oath; or goes to the duel; or deposits the value before the cross.

ARTICLE 18. And if a purchasing agent or a dealer in cattle traveling in a country district sues another for storage of grain or of other goods, the court, after having the matter justly examined, leaves the procedure to the defendant's will: if he wants it, he takes the oath; or goes to the duel; or deposits [the value] before the cross.

ARTICLE 19. And if anyone sues another for goods in storage on the evidence of [noncertified] notes, or without producing an itemized list of goods stored, or after the expiration of term agreed upon, he loses the suit.

ARTICLE 20. And if anyone sues another for beating or robbery [and produces a witness], the prince and the mayor, and the hundreders have to inquire of the witness where he dined and where he lodged the night [of the crime]; and whether he happened to be a co-lodger or a co-diner [of the litigants]; likewise they have to inquire of the beaten man where the beating and robbery took place and before whom he declared it. He must refer to someone specifically. And if the man referred to appears before the court and

---

ARTICLES 16 and 17. The text of both articles is incomplete. It is obvious that we have here two versions of a similar clause, based in each case upon a law passed by the Pskov city assembly, or upon different records of Pskov customary law.

ARTICLE 18. "Purchasing agent," *zakupen;* "dealer in cattle," *skotnik.* Cherepnin and Iakovlev interpret these terms differently: according to them, *zakupen* would be a "migratory laborer"; such laborer may either till the land or tend cattle; in the latter case he would be called *skotnik*, from *skot*, cattle. This interpretation seems forced to me.

ARTICLE 20. "Witness," here and hereafter, *poslukh.*

declares justly, as if facing God, that the offended man made a deposition about his beating and robbery; and the witness, standing before the court, confirms the statement, then the court leaves the procedure to the defendant's will: if he desires, he goes to the duel against the witness; or he deposits [the amount of damages] before a cross in the presence of the witness.

ARTICLE 21. And if [in a duel] the opponent of the witness is an old man or a youth, or a cripple, or a priest, or a monk, he may hire a fighter [as his substitute] against the witness; and the witness has no right to hire a substitute.

ARTICLE 22. And if a claimant refers to a witness, and that witness does not appear before the court, or having appeared omits or adds anything to the required form of deposition, such witness is not a witness, and the plaintiff loses the suit.

ARTICLE 23. And if the plaintiff produces a witness and the defendant says thus, "The plaintiff himself beat me assisted by that witness and now he produces him as the witness," [such witness is not a witness]. Only a witness recognized as such by the court may serve as a witness.

ARTICLE 24. And again, if the defendant produces no witness, the plaintiff is not entitled to produce a witness either. In such cases the court appoints men [to examine the case]. And the claimant who produced no witness should not be accused on the ground that he did not produce a witness. In Pskov the supreme court disregards such accusation.

ARTICLE 25. And if the constable summons a claimant to the court and the claimant does not come to the church square to read the summons, then the summons is to be read in the church square in the presence of a priest; or again, if the one on whom summons has been served, disregarding the term appointed, does not appear before the supreme court, [the judge], after five days following the expiration of the term, issues a writ against the claimant [who disregarded the summons, and a copy of the writ is given to the other claimant].

ARTICLE 26. And when the claimant who has received a copy of the writ against his contestant seizes the latter he must not inflict pain on him nor beat him, but must bring him to the court. And the defendant against whom the writ has been issued must not fight his opponent or pierce him [with any weapon]; and if he fights him or pierces him and kills him, he is subject to prosecution as a murderer.

CHARTER OF PSKOV 67

ARTICLE 27. And if a fight takes place in the market place or in a street, be it in Pskov or in a borough, or in a village in a country district, or at a banquet, but there is no robbery, and many people happen to witness that fight either in the market place, or in the street, or at the banquet, and four or five men appear before us [the court] and say, "He beat that man," then that man who beat the offended is surrendered to him; and the fine to the prince is collected. And if the beaten man accuses his offender of robbery, he may start a lawsuit producing one witness; the duel may be ordered in such a case.

ARTICLE 28. And if anyone sues another for the money he loaned on the evidence of a [noncertified] note and, in addition, produces a security; then it is left to the will of the plaintiff: if he wishes, he may take the oath and [if the validity of his oath is recognized by the court] receive his money back; and if he wishes, he deposits the pledge before the cross; and the defendant kisses the cross and [if the court is satisfied] receives his pledge back; and the duel is not ordered when there is a pledge: pledge certificates are not to be disregarded.

ARTICLE 29. If a man gives another a pawn as security for the loan [he received]—deeds or any valuables—and then seizes his creditor or brings him to the court by surprise, and the creditor holding the pledge has no certificate about him, he does not stand accused because of it but has to be trusted, if only he produces the pledge. The court leaves it to the will of the one who produced the pledge: if he wishes, he takes the oath concerning the money [he loaned]; or he deposits the pledge before the cross; and [the debtor] after having kissed the cross, [if the court is satisfied] receives his pledge back.

ARTICLE 30. And if anyone intends to loan money [to another], he may lend up to one ruble without a pledge and without a [certified] note, but no money to the amount over one ruble should be lent without security and without a note. And if anyone sues for his money for the amount over one ruble on the evidence of a [noncertified] note, holding no pledge, his note is invalid, and the defendant wins the case.

ARTICLE 31. If anyone sues another man for money lent on the basis of a [noncertified] note, and in addition produces a pledge—be it clothes, or armor, or a horse, or any movables—but the value is less than that of the loan, [then], if the defendant denies that that is his pledge and says thus, "I did not deposit any security with thee and did not accept any loan from thee," the plaintiff keeps the pledge, and the defendant stands cleared.

ARTICLE 32. If any man vouches for another in the latter's loan and the creditor sues the guarantor for his money, and the defendant [for whom the other man vouched] produces the creditor's receipt and says thus, "Brother, I paid thee the money vouched for, here is the receipt according to which the creditor is not to sue either the debtor or the guarantor for the money"; and if there is no copy of that receipt in the files [at the Holy Trinity Cathedral] the receipt is not valid, and the creditor may sue the guarantor for his money.

ARTICLE 33. And loans may be guaranteed to the amount of one ruble, and [no guaranty is accepted] over one ruble.

ARTICLE 34. And if a Pskov citizen's property is stolen, be it in Pskov, or in a borough, or in a village in a country district, he must declare it before the elders, or the neighbors, or other men not related to him; and at a banquet, before the steward, or the convives; but the chairman of the banquet is not . . . ; and in a country district the Pskov citizen must not compel all of the villagers to come to take oath at Pskov . . . ; but he shall bring to the oath him only against whom he has a specific suspicion.

ARTICLE 35. If a theft has been committed, the robbed man should not summon men [outside of the quarters where the theft has taken place]: not those who are in church, nor [all] of the borough inhabitants or villagers staying in a borough, nor those in the market place; but he summons to the oath only those who happen to be near the place of the theft.

ARTICLE 36. And if a woman sues a man for debts on the evidence of [noncertified] notes, or a child, or an old man, or a sick person, or a cripple, or a monk, or a nun, each of them may hire a substitute

---

ARTICLES 34 and 35. The text, in the original, is very unclear. Cherepnin and Iakovlev combine the two articles into one. The meaning of the clause, according to them, is that of a Pskov citizen may not summon the suspected villager to Pskov for the trial, and a villager, in case *he* suspects a Pskov citizen in theft, may not summon him to the village. In Article 34, "country district," *volost'*; "banquet," *pir*. "Banquet" was a peculiar social institution in medieval Russian cities. In Pskov, as in Novgorod, there existed special "banquet fraternities" (*bratchina*, see Article 113 below), usually connected with a merchant or an artisan guild.

fighter [for the duel]; and the plaintiff kisses the cross, but fights [the duel] through his substitute; and the defendant may hire a fighter of his against the plaintiff's fighter, or fight him personally.

ARTICLE 37. If the court orders that the litigation be decided by a duel, and the plaintiff overcomes the defendant on the duelling grounds, he receives the amount for which he sued; [in case the defendant is killed], the victor must not claim any redemption money for the body [of the vanquished from the latter's relatives]; he may only take the armor [of the vanquished], or any equipment he fought in. And the culprit's side pays the fine to the prince and the constable's fees to two constables, 6 *denga* each, in case the duel has actually taken place; if the contestants settle their claims on the ground before the duel has taken place, 3 *denga* to each of the two constables. If the plaintiff loses, the fine to the prince is not collected.

ARTICLE 38. If anyone sues another for money he loaned him for commercial transactions on the basis of [noncertified] notes, and the defendant produces a receipt in which it is mentioned that the money loaned to him for commerce [has been paid by him], but there is no copy of the receipt in the files at the Holy Trinity Cathedral, the receipt is not valid.

ARTICLE 39. And if a master carpenter or a hired craftsman accomplishes the work [and the employer refuses to pay him], he may sue the employer for his pay through an announcement [in the market place].

ARTICLE 40. And if a hired worker about the homestead leaves his employer before the completion of his appointed work, he receives wages in accordance with the amount [of time he worked]. And a worker may sue his employer for his wages only within one year after his leaving the work; if he stayed with his employer for five or ten years and did not receive his wages, he may claim his wages for all that period. But after the expiration of one year [after the worker's discharge] a worker may not sue his employer.

ARTICLE 41. And if a hired carpenter sues his employer for his wages, and that carpenter has left without having completed his work; and if [facing the court], the carpenter says to his employer, "I have completed all my work for thee"; and the employer says, "Thou hast not completed thy work"—then, if there has been no written agreement between them, the employer shall deposit the amount sued for before the cross, [letting the employee take the oath]; or the employer himself takes the oath.

ARTICLE 42. And if the landlord wants to terminate the lease of his tenant farmer, or vegetable gardener, or fisherman, the term for ending such leases is the day of the beginning of St. Philip's fast; likewise, if the farmer wants to terminate the lease on the farm, or the vegetable gardener, or the fisherman [wants to terminate the lease], the term is the same, and there shall be no other term, either for the landlord, or for the farmer, or the fisherman, or the vegetable gardener. And if the farmer, or the vegetable gardener, or the fisherman refuses to leave because of the [unlawful] term set by the landlord, he wins, and the landlord loses his customary quarter [of farm products], or his portion of the vegetables, or his portion of fish from the fishery.

ARTICLE 43. And if a lessee of a fishery misses the spring catch of fish, he shall pay the landlord according to the yield the landlord got from his other fisheries.

ARTICLE 44. And at the termination of the lease, either by the landlord or by the lessee, the landlord may sue his farmer, or vegetable gardener, or fisherman for the amount of money or grain [he may have loaned him], stating kinds of grain, specifically, such as spring wheat, or winter wheat, through an announcement in the market place.

ARTICLE 45. And whoever sues for money loaned for commercial transactions, or for money guaranteed [by the co-maker of the loan], or for goods placed in storage, or for money loaned for business purpose, or for his deceased relative's estate, and fails to state the amount of his claims by items, he loses the suit.

ARTICLE 46. And if a man [from whom something was stolen] finds the object at some other man's house, and this latter says [to the judge] thus, "I have bought it at the market but cannot identify the man from whom I bought it," the defendant must take the oath that he bought the object honestly at the market and was not a party to the theft. Even though he does not produce the man [from whom he bought the object], if he never had been accused of theft and there is no suspicion against him, the plaintiff loses his claim [for damages].

ARTICLE 42. "Tenant-farmer," *izornik*; "vegetable gardener," *ogorodnik*; "fisherman," *kochetnik*, a dialect term. St. Philip's day, November 14. "Fishery," *isad*.

ARTICLE 47. And if anyone buys anything in a foreign land or a foreign city, or finds anything anywhere, and another man claims it as his property, the procedure is like [that in the case of a stolen object bought] at the market place.

ARTICLE 48. And if anyone sues an official [demanding that the latter refund the amount unlawfully extorted from the plaintiff] as remuneration, and [upon the examination of the case it is revealed that the official] forcibly seized [the plaintiff's] clothes or horse saying, "I take the clothes, or the horse, on account of the promised [remuneration]," the culprit stands guilty of robbery.

ARTICLE 49. And the prince's men and [city] constables shall travel in pairs; and their allowance for travel expenses is one *denga* for each ten versts; the amount is the same whether two or three of them travel. And if the prince's man or the constable refuses to travel for that allowance, the Pskov citizen [for the examination of whose suit the officials travel] may send anyone within the same allowance.

ARTICLE 50. And the prince's scribe shall collect his fee for his writing a summons, or a writ, or an order to the constable [to accompany the claimant], in accordance with the plaintiff's paying capacity. And if he claims a fee above the plaintiff's capacity, the latter may have the document written anywhere [by a private scribe] and let the prince seal it; and if the prince will not seal the document, it may be sealed at the Holy Trinity Cathedral; there is no offense in it.

ARTICLE 51. And if a farmer denies that he owes any money to his landlord and says thus, "I stayed on thy land, but owe thee nothing," the landlord must produce some outsiders, four or five of them, and those men must state the case justly as if facing God. [And if they say] that the farmer did occupy the plot [presumably receiving a subsidy from the lord], then it is left to the landlord's will: he may take the oath and then [if the court is satisfied] receive the subsidy back; or the farmer takes the oath. And if the landlord produces no men [to confirm the fact] that the farmer stayed on his land [receiving a subsidy], he loses [the right to claim back] the subsidy.

ARTICLE 48. The translation is according to Cherepnin and Iakovlev.

ARTICLE 49. "Constable," *podvoisky*, a city official. Note that the prince's agents must be accompanied by city officials.

ARTICLE 51. "Subsidy," *pokruta*. A tenant farmer in Pskov usually received from the owner of the land an amount of money, or seeds. He had to return it upon leaving.

ARTICLE 52. And in litigations about theft and robbery the prince's fine is in proportion only to that part of the plaintiff's claims which has been recognized as valid.

ARTICLE 53. If any son leaves [his parents'] home and fails to feed his father and mother until their death, he has no portion in their estate.

ARTICLE 54. If the man [in whose possession something claimed as stolen is found by its owner] brings to the court or puts to oath the man from whom he bought that object, then the plaintiff who searched for the object and had it enjoined may sue the seller, and the holder of the object vouches for the seller's appearance before the court.

ARTICLE 55. If anyone claims another's property which the latter inherited from his father [intestate], or which was bequeathed to him by his father, and the neighbors as well as outsiders know about it, and four or five of them stand before the court and state justly, as if facing God, that that property has been indeed inherited by the defendant or bequeathed to him by his father, then the defendant is not required to take the oath and the plaintiff loses. But if there are not four or five men who will make the statement about the case justly, as if facing God, then the defendant must take the oath [to prove] that the property sued for has been inherited by him from his father.

ARTICLE 56. And likewise if anyone bought something at the market but cannot identify the man from whom he bought it, and another man claims [that it is an object stolen from him], and there are reliable people who know [that the defendant actually bought the object], and four or five of them state justly, as if facing God, "He bought it at the market in our presence," the defendant is right and need not take the oath. But if he cannot produce any eyewitnesses he must take the oath, and [if the court is satisfied] the plaintiff loses.

ARTICLE 57. And if anyone asks the prince or the mayor to assign to him constables for the investigation of a theft, the prince and the mayor must assign worthy and reliable men; and those constables conduct the investigation at the spot of the theft. And if the con-

---

ARTICLE 57. "Constable," *pristav*, who might be either a prince's or a city official.

stables report as follows, "We came to the [suspected] house for the investigation of the theft, and that man objected to the investigation, and did not let us inside the house, and chased us from his homestead"; and if the man who was to be examined says thus, "My lords, those constables did not call on me," or he says thus, "Those constables called on me and I opened the house for them, but they did not examine me and of their own will left my homestead and now maliciously slander me"; in such case the prince and the mayor shall question the constables thus, "Have you any eyewitnesses in the presence of whom that man chased you from his homestead?" Then the constables have to produce two or three men, and if those men stand before the court and state justly as if facing God, "It is in our presence that that man refused to let the constables examine him and chased them from his homestead," the constables are right and that man is to be prosecuted for theft. But if [the eyewitnesses do not confirm the constables' report], those constables are no constables, and the plaintiff who used their services loses his suit.

ARTICLE 58. And no assistant [to either of the litigants] is allowed in the court; only the two contestants enter the court hall and neither of them can bring any attorney. Only in case [the contestant] is a woman, or a child, or a monk, or a nun, or a very old man, or a deaf man, he, or she, may bring his or her attorney along. And except in those cases no attorney is allowed, and if one forces his way into the court hall, or strikes the porter, he is to be put in stocks and must pay one ruble fine to the prince and 10 *denga* to the porters.

ARTICLE 59. And the porters shall serve in pairs, one being appointed by the prince and the other by the city of Pskov, and they have to swear that they will not ruin the innocent, nor help the guilty one. And from each case tried in the court the two of them receive one *denga* from the guilty party.

ARTICLE 60. And the thief's deposition is to be examined. If he informs against anyone, that man's house must be searched, and, if they find there the stolen object, [the owner of the house] is considered a thief; and if they find nothing in his house, he is left free.

ARTICLE 61. And neither the prince nor the mayor may order a new trial for lawsuit on which there is already a copy of the court decision. But if there is a suspicion that that copy be a forgery, the matter is reëxamined by the court.

ARTICLE 62. If anyone sues another man for something on the

evidence of [noncertified] notes or a security, and then, at the court or at the administering of the oath, comes to an agreement with the defendant [decreasing the amount of his claims], there is no fine for it. The plaintiff may even excuse the defendant from any reimbursement without bringing him to the oath.

ARTICLE 63. And if a tenant farmer terminates the lease on his farm, or the landlord terminates it, the landlord receives half of the harvest and the farmer the other half.

ARTICLE 64. And if any constable, be he the prince's man or Pskov's man, is sent to serve the summons on a defendant, or to put a defendant in shackles, or to take shackles off, his allowance for travel expenses is one *denga* for each ten versts.

ARTICLE 65. And if a constable is sent to examine a theft, his allowance is doubled and is paid by the guilty party. And if he fails to find the stolen object, then [the plaintiff] who commissioned the constable pays both the constable's and the porter's fees.

ARTICLE 66. And when a constable, or a squire, confiscates [the defendant's] horse or anything else, he must hand it to an outsider [for safe keeping]; but if no outsider agrees to keep it, he himself takes it along. The constable's travel expenses are paid by the loser of the suit.

ARTICLE 67. And if the plaintiff, traveling with the constable, takes anything by force [from the defendant] to reimburse himself, and then fails to prove his claims against the defendant, he is prosecuted for robbery. And the fine in robbery cases is one ruble; the fine, as well as the constable's fee, to be paid by the guilty party.

ARTICLE 68. And no mayor may be an attorney in another's lawsuit, but can only be [a litigant] in his own lawsuit, or an attorney in a lawsuit involving the church of which he is warden.

ARTICLE 69. And no other public official may serve as an attorney for another [citizen], but only [a litigant] in his own lawsuit.

ARTICLE 70. And in the litigations about church land the neighbors are not allowed to enter the court hall; only the churchwardens are admitted.

ARTICLE 71. And one attorney may not conduct two lawsuits in the same day.

ARTICLE 72. And if [a plot of land or a fishery establishment] is

---

ARTICLE 66. "Squire," *dvorianin*. See note to Article 3, p. 58.

bequeathed to anyone for his use, and he [fraudulently] obtains deeds to that land or fishery establishment and sells that land or fishery establishment or whatever it be and is detected, he must redeem that land or fishery establishment or whatever it be, and besides he has forfeited his use of the property.

ARTICLE 73. And if a creditor has a note [on a loan], and the amount of interest agreed upon is stated in the note, and he presents the note to the court in time [as agreed upon] he receives the interest; but if he fails to present to the court his claim in time, he receives no interest.

ARTICLE 74. If the creditor demands his money back before the expiration of the term [of the loan], he may not claim the interest. And if the debtor wants to return the loan before the expiration of its term he pays the interest in proportion to the time used.

ARTICLE 75. And if a tenant farmer sues his landlord on the evidence of a [noncertified] note, that note is invalid.

ARTICLE 75A. And if the farmer is an old tenant, he may sue his landlord.

ARTICLE 76. And if a tenant farmer leaves his farm [illegally] and goes abroad or anywhere, and there are some movables of his left on the farm, and the landlord wants to have his subsidy [to that

---

ARTICLE 75A. The meaning of this clause has become the subject of a protracted controversy among students of Russian legal history. The text seems to be corrupted. The manuscript reads: *vozi vesti na gosudaria*, literally "to drive wagons for the landlord." Some scholars, as for example M. A. Diakonov, and recently Cherepnin and Iakovlev, are ready to accept the text as it is. They interpret the clause as imposing on the old tenants an additional obligation—that of driving the landlord's wagons. However, such a clause would seem entirely out of place here. F. Ustrialov suggested (in 1855) the reading *vozvesti* instead of *vozi vesti*. He understood the clause in the sense that an old tenant was entitled to bring accusations against the landlord. *Vozvesti* would be, however, an unusual term in this connotation. In my opinion, we have here a case of copyist's mistake; in the original copy of the charter, the clause must have been worded differently. I suggest reading *volno sochiti* or *volno iskati* (instead of *vozi vesti*) : *A staromu izorniku volno sochiti na gosudari* ("And if a farmer is an old tenant, he may sue his landlord"). For terminological analogy, see the Russian text at the end of Article 76: *a izorniku na gosudari zhivota ne sochiti* ("and the farmer may not sue the landlord for his movables") ; and at the end of Article 86: *volno iskati u gosudaria* ("they may sue the landlord for it"), Article 75A, as emendated, may be interpreted in two different ways. If we admit, with

farmer] refunded, he shall ask the prince and the mayor for constables and shall call district elders and outsiders, and shall sell the farmer's movables in the presence of the officials and the outsiders, and receive his money back out of the proceeds [of the sales]. And if the amount of the subsidy is not covered and, later on, the farmer appears, the landlord may sue him for the balance of the subsidy; and the landlord is not liable to any fine [for selling the farmer's property]; and the farmer may not sue the landlord for his property [sold by the latter].

ARTICLE 77. And the Pskov judges, and the borough mayors, and the elders must swear that they will conduct the trials justly in accordance with their oaths; and if they fail to conduct the trials justly, God will be their judge on the fateful day of Christ's second advent.

ARTICLE 78. And when the prince's man proceeds to the examination of contested boundaries of a landed estate, together with the hundreders, he likewise has to kiss the cross.

ARTICLE 79. And if there is litigation about land and water, and two deeds are produced, the prince's secretary shall read one deed and the city secretary shall read the other. And if a deed certified in a borough is produced, the city secretary shall read it.

ARTICLE 80. And if a fight occurs—be it in Pskov, or in a borough, or in a country district, at a banquet, or anywhere—and the constables are not called, and the adversaries apologize mutually, the fine to the prince is not collected.

ARTICLE 81. And the prince's men and the Pskov officials, when sent as constables or for examination of eyewitnesses, shall travel in pairs.

ARTICLE 82. And when the prince's scribe writes a copy of the court decision concerning land, his fee is five *denga;* and for writing a summons, one *denga;* and for sealing a document, one *denga;* and for writing a writ, or an order to the constables [to accompany the

---

Diakonov and some other scholars, that an old tenant was considered under a greater obligation to the lord than a new tenant, the clause would mean that *even* an old tenant farmer was entitled to sue the lord (if he had a better evidence than noncertified notes). However, it may be argued that in Pskov an old tenant might have been considered a more reliable man than a new tenant. In such a case, the clause would mean that an old tenant was entitled to sue the lord even on the basis of noncertified notes. This second explanation seems more plausible to me.

plaintiff], one *denga*. And if the prince's scribe refuses to write [any of these documents] for the prescribed fee, the claimant may have the document written elsewhere [by a private scribe] and have it sealed by the prince; and if the prince refuses to seal it, it may be sealed at the Holy Trinity Cathedral; there is no offense in it.

ARTICLE 83. And when a Pskov citizen applies to the prince for a passport to travel abroad on his own business, the prince's scribe shall collect one *denga* [for writing the passport]; and one *denga* for sealing it.

ARTICLE 84. And if a tenant farmer dies and there is no wife, or children, or a brother, or any relative left, the landlord is entitled to sell the movables in order to recover his subsidy; [and if] later on any descendants of the deceased, or a brother of his, appear, they may not sue the landlord for [the tenant's] movables.

ARTICLE 85. And if a tenant farmer dies, and the landlord has his note on the subsidy, and if there are wife and children left, even if they have not been mentioned in the note [as co-makers] they may not deny their liability but must repay the subsidy according to the note. And if there is no note, the case is tried according to the Pskov customary law.

ARTICLE 86. And if after a tenant farmer's death his brother or other descendants are left and claim his movables, the landlord may sue them for the subsidy [previously accepted by the deceased]. [On the other hand], the brother and descendants of the deceased may not hold the landlord responsible for the loss of a basket or a keg; but as to a horse, or a cow, they may sue the landlord for it.

ARTICLE 87. And if a tenant farmer sues the landlord for some movables and the landlord supplies sufficient evidence that the object in question [is his own property], and it is known to outsiders as well as to the neighbors that the object belongs to the landlord, then the tenant loses the suit, and the landlord is right.

ARTICLE 88. And if a man's wife dies without a will, and there is some landed property of hers left, the husband may possess that property until his death, provided he does not marry again; but if he marries, he loses the use of the property.

ARTICLE 89. And if a woman's husband dies without a will, and there is some landed or movable próperty of his left, his wife has the use of the property until her death provided she does not marry again; and if she marries, she loses the use of the property.

ARTICLE 90. And if a man's wife dies, and the husband marries again, and the wife's mother, or sister, or other relatives, claim her clothes, the husband must honestly, in accordance with his conscience, hand them her clothes, but he is not required to take the oath [to prove] that there are no more of her clothes left. Similarly, if the husband dies, and his father or brothers claim his clothes, his widow must honestly, in accordance with her conscience, hand them whatever [personal belongings] are left from her husband, but she is not required to take the oath [to prove] that there are no more clothes left.

ARTICLE 91. And if a man's son dies and there is a daughter-in-law left, and she claims her jewels or clothes from her father-in-law, or her brother-in-law, the father-in-law, or the brother-in-law, has to hand her the clothes or jewels. But if the daughter-in-law presents false claims, then the procedure is left to the father-in-law's, or brother-in-law's, will: if he wishes, he takes the oath; or he deposits the object in question before the cross.

ARTICLE 92. And if anyone sues another for his share in a coöperative corporation—this clause does not apply to money loaned for commercial transactions or for interest—and produces a [noncertified] receipt, the procedure is left to the defendant's will: if he wishes, he takes the oath; or deposits [the value] before the cross; or resorts to the duel.

ARTICLE 93. And if a debtor [in a loan on which the creditor has] a certified note, or a tenant farmer under similar conditions, hides from the creditor and fails to appear before the court at the expiration of the term [of the loan] and there are expenses, such as the constable's fees, or the fine [for not obeying the court's order], or the fee for shackling [the delinquent]—all that is to be paid by the guilty party.

ARTICLE 94. And if the elder brother lives in the same household with his younger brother, and anyone sues them for their father's debts but cannot produce the father's certified note, then the elder brother has to swear [that the debt is his father's and not his] and the debt is paid out of the common property of the brothers and they divide the balance as they please.

ARTICLE 92. "Share in a coöperative corporation," *siabrenoe serebro*, literally, "coöperative funds." *Siabr*, co-owner, see Article 106.

ARTICLE 95. And if a younger brother, or a nephew, lives in the same household with his elder brother, or his uncle, and appropriates some valuables of his brother, or his uncle, and denies it, he must swear [that what he took was his share], and the estate shall then be divided.

ARTICLE 96. And if a murder is committed and the murderer is detected, the prince collects from him one ruble fine.

ARTICLE 97. And if it is the son who killed his father, or the brother his brother, the fine to the prince is collected just the same.

ARTICLE 98. And if a claimant accompanied by a constable comes to another's homestead to arrest a thief, or to examine a theft, or to arrest a debtor, and a woman [in that household] miscarries and charges the constable, or the claimant, with murder [of her child], there is no murder in it.

ARTICLE 99. And if any defendant fails to appear to take the judicial oath [at the appointed time], he is not admitted to the oath [after the expiration of the term] and has to pay the damages in full.

ARTICLE 100. And if a man, during his life, or on his deathbed, gives with his own hand to any relative his clothes, or any movables, or lands, or deeds, in the presence of a priest, or outsiders, the recipient of the gift shall own it, even if there is no will left.

ARTICLE 101. *On commercial loans and on guarantee.* And if anyone sues another for money loaned to the latter for commercial transactions, or sues the guarantor on the loan, the procedure is left to the defendant's will: if he wishes, he goes to the duel; or he deposits the value before the cross.

ARTICLE 102. And if a master sues his apprentice for his fee, and the apprentice denies [that he owes anything to the master], the procedure is left to the master's will: if he wishes, he takes the oath; or they let the apprentice take the oath.

ARTICLE 103. And a lodger may sue his landlord for money loaned or for any other cause.

ARTICLE 103A. And if anyone conducts litigation against another on the basis of a certified note, or a pledge as evidence of obligation, and the obligor [in his turn] sues the obligee for money loaned, or for goods in storage, or for anything else, on the evidence of a [non-certified] note, or a note on commercial loan, the case is tried by the court in accordance with Pskov customary law.

ARTICLE 104. And if, [after anybody's death], two, or three, or five claimants on the estate of the deceased produce deeds [accepted by them as security] on the same plot of land or water, or the same homestead, or the same barn, and some of the claimants have deeds accepted by them as security and in addition have notes and pledge certificates, and the others have no notes, only deeds accepted as security, these latter have to take the oath, and then the property of the deceased is divided among all of the claimants in proportion to the amount of each claim; and if any close relatives [of the deceased] want to redeem a pledge, they pay accordingly. And when a claimant has a pledge or a note on the estate of the deceased, he is not required to take the oath.

ARTICLE 105. And if a foreigner sues [a native] for damages in a beating or robbery, the procedure is left to the defendant's will: if he wishes, he takes the oath [to prove] that he did not beat or rob [the foreigner]; or he deposits the amount sued for before the cross.

ARTICLE 106. And if there is litigation about a landed property, or an apiary, and [the defendant] produces his old deed, and [the plaintiff] produces his [more recent] deed of sale, and if that deed affects many co-owners of the land, or of the apiary, and they all appear before the court, defending each his share of the land, or of the apiary, and present to the supreme court their [old] deeds and then call land surveyors, and the latter, taking into account old men's assertions, establish their boundaries, the plaintiff shall take the oath [to prove] that the contestable portion of the land duly belongs to him. [If the plaintiff lets the defendants take the oath], only one of the co-owners takes the oath in the name of all of them; and that one receives a copy of the court decision.

ARTICLE 107. And if anyone gives [to his creditor] some object as security [on the loan] and at the expiration of the term wants to repay the loan and claims back the object pledged, and [the creditor] denies the existence of the transaction and says thus, "I have not loaned any money to thee, nor have I accepted any pledge from thee," the court allows the defendant to choose one of the three methods of procedure as follows: if he wishes, he takes the oath [to

---

ARTICLE 106. "Co-owners," *siabry* (plural from *siabr*). This is a case of a litigation between an individual landowner and a group of coöperative owners.

prove] that he accepted no pledge; or he deposits the value of the pledge in cash before the cross; or he goes to the duel.

ARTICLE 108. And if any provision of the customary law is missing in this charter, the mayor may refer the matter to Lord Pskov at the city assembly, advising the insertion of a new clause accordingly. And if any clause in this charter is not satisfactory to Lord Pskov, that clause is to be deleted.

ARTICLE 109. And the priests, and the deacons, and the woman baker of the ritual bread, and the monk, and the nun, are tried by the archbishop's lieutenant. If a priest, or a deacon, sues a monk, or a nun, that is when both litigants are churchmen, the prince, or the mayor, or the [city] judges may not try them, since they are liable to the court of the archbishop's lieutenant. But if one of the litigants is [a churchman] and the other is a layman, and not both of them churchmen, then the prince, or the mayor, or the [city] judges shall try their cases in a joint session with the archbishop's lieutenant.

ARTICLE 110. If they sue a man for a horse, or a cow, or any other animal even if it be a dog, and the defendant says, "It is my own, bred on my place," he has to swear that the animal is bred on his place.

ARTICLE 111. And if anyone strikes his contestant in the court hall, he shall be turned over to the offended man for the payment of one ruble, and besides he shall pay a fine to the prince.

ARTICLE 112. And [in litigations about domestic animals and poultry] the payments are set as follows: to the owner, for the ram, 6 *denga*, for the ewe, 10 *denga*; and to the judge, 3 *denga*, according to the old custom. And for the gander and for the goose, for each, 2 *denga* to the owner and 3 *denga* to the judge; and for the duck and for the drake, and for the rooster and for the hen, 2 *denga*.

ARTICLE 113. And the fraternity has judicial authority [over its members].

ARTICLE 114. And if two men, both being drunk, exchange some things, or one of them sells anything to the other, and then, after they sleep their drunkenness off, one of them is not satisfied with the deal, they may change the things back; and no oath is required in such a case, and there is no fine.

ARTICLE 113. "Fraternity," *bratchina*. See note to Article 34.

ARTICLE 115. And the prince's men may not keep taverns either in Pskov, or in a borough, nor sell mead by pails, or by dippers, or by kegs.

ARTICLE 116. And if anyone sues another for arson, and there is no evidence, the defendant may be acquitted by his taking the oath.

ARTICLE 117. And if anyone tears another's beard, and there is a witness, that witness shall take the oath and go to the duel against the defendant, and if the witness wins, the amend for the tearing of the beard is two rubles and there is the princely fine besides. And only one witness is admitted.

ARTICLE 118. And if anyone buys a cow at a price agreed upon, and after the purchase [the cow gives birth to a calf], the seller may not sue the buyer for that calf; [on the other hand], if the cow discharges bloody urine, it may be returned and the money is to be refunded.

ARTICLE 119. And a duel may be ordered between two women but neither may hire a substitute.

ARTICLE 120. [And if a fight occurs] and five men, or ten, or any number of them, sue five other men, or one man, for bruises, and win, the payment for the offense is one ruble collectively—from all of the defendants to all of the plaintiffs. And only one fine is collected [and paid] to the prince.

THE CHARTER OF THE CITY OF NOVGOROD

[PREAMBLE]. Having referred the matter to the Lords—the Grand Dukes—Grand Duke Ivan Vasilievich, of all Russia, and his son, Grand Duke Ivan Ivanovich, for their approval, and having received the blessing of the Archbishop-elect of Novgorod the Great and Pskov, Hieromonk Theophilus, we, the mayors of Novgorod, and the chiliarchs of Novgorod, and the boyars, and the middle-class burghers, and the merchants, and the lower-class burghers, all the five city districts, the whole Sovereign Novgorod the Great, at the city assembly in the Iaroslav Square, have completed and confirmed the following:

ARTICLE 1. The Archbishop-elect of Novgorod the Great and Pskov, Hieromonk Theophilus, in his court—the ecclesiastical court —shall conduct trials in accordance with the rules of the holy fathers —the Nomocanon; and he shall give equal justice to every litigant, be he a boyar, or a middle-class burgher, or a lower-class burgher.

Note. Vladimirsky-Budanov's edition has been used for this translation. The division into articles is also Vladimirsky-Budanov's.

PREAMBLE. Grand Duke Ivan Vasilievich (Ivan III) was the son of Vasili II and the grandson of Vasili I, the grantor of the Dvina Land charter. Ivan Ivanovich, son of Ivan III, was a Grand Duke by title only. He did not reign, since he died before his father. Theophilus was formally installed as Archbishop of Novgorod only after the promulgation of the charter. Mayor, *posadnik*. Even after the expiration of their term in office the Novgorod mayors kept their title and enjoyed considerable influence in city affairs. The same is true of the chiliarch (*tysiatsky;* see Introduction, Section IV, p. 18). "Middle-class burghers," *zhit'i liudi* (literally, "well-to-do men"). "Lower-class burghers," *chernye liudi* (literally, "black men"). "City district," *konets.* City assembly, *veche.* Note the title of the commonwealth of Novgorod: *Gosudar' Veliky Novgorod* ("Sovereign Novgorod the Great"). For the historical background, see Introduction, Section IV, p. 19.

ARTICLE 1. "Lower-class burgher," in this case, *molodchi chelovek,* literally "younger man."

ARTICLE 2. And the mayor in his court shall conduct trials jointly with the Grand Duke's lieutenants, according to the old customs; and without the concurrency of the Grand Duke's lieutenants the mayor may not conclude any lawsuit.

ARTICLE 3. And the Grand Duke's lieutenants and justices have authority to reëxamine causes in appeal proceedings, according to the old customs.

ARTICLE 4. And the chiliarch conducts trials in his court. And all of them must conduct trials justly according to their oath.

ARTICLE 5. And each contestant may elect two assessors to sit in the court. And once the assessor is chosen by the contestant, he must continue to deal with him. But the authority of the mayor, and the chiliarch, and the archbishop's lieutenant, and their judges, in the conduct of the trials, must not be interfered with.

ARTICLE 6. And the litigant must not bring along with him his partisans for intimidating the other litigant, or the mayor, or the chiliarch, or the archbishop's lieutenant, or other judges, or the members of the Court of Reëxamination. And whoever brings his partisans for intimidating the mayor, or the chiliarch, or the archbishop's lieutenant, or other judges, or the members of the Court of Reëxamination, or the other litigant, be it at the trial, or at the reëxamination of the case, or on the duel field, stands guilty, and the Grand Dukes and Novgorod the Great fine the culprit for bringing his partisans to the amount, as follows: the boyar, 50 rubles; the middle-class burgher, 20 rubles; the lower-class burgher, 10 rubles; and besides he pays damages to the other litigant.

ARTICLE 7. And if anyone wants to sue for a landed estate—for a farm homestead, or two of them, or more, or less—he may not, prior to the court proceedings, come to the land or send his men there [in an attempt to seize it by force], but must refer the matter to the court. And if he wins the suit, he receives from the judge a copy of the court decision assigning the land to him and entitling him to collect damages from the defendant. And the judge may not claim any taxes [but only the customary court fees].

ARTICLE 3. The Grand Duke's justices, *tiuny*, plural from *tiun* (see the Russian Law, Short Version, note to Article 22, p. 31). Appeal proceedings and the "Court of Appeals," *peresud*.

ARTICLE 6. The "Court of Reëxamination," *doklad*; member of such Court, *dokladchik*.

ARTICLE 8. And out of each ruble of court fees the archbishop, or his lieutenant, and the sealer receive one *grivna*; and out of the fees on writs [issued without a trial because of the failure of one of the defendants to appear before the court], of each ruble the archbishop, or his lieutenant, and the sealer receive 3 *denga*. And the mayor and the chiliarch, and their judges, and the borough judges, receive out of each ruble of court fees 7 *denga*, and out of each ruble of writ fees, 3 *denga*.

ARTICLE 9. And the mayor, and the chiliarch, and the archbishop's lieutenant, and their judges, and the borough judges shall complete the conduct of each trial within a month; and they may not prolong the conduct of any case beyond that term.

ARTICLE 10. And if anyone sues another for the forcible seizure and robbery of his land, the court tries first the case about the forcible seizure and robbery and then about [the ownership of] the land. And whoever is accused in the forcible seizure of land and robbery, the Grand Dukes and Novgorod the Great fine the culprit to the amount as follows: the boyar, 50 rubles; the middle-class burgher, 20 rubles; and the lower-class burgher, 10 rubles. Then the lawsuit about [the ownership of] land is tried. And even if that latter suit is postponed [for any reason] by the Novgorod court, the case about the forcible seizure is tried just the same.

ARTICLE 11. And if a litigant wishes to sue his contestant simultaneously for forcible seizure and robbery, and for assertion of ownership, the contestant must produce his counterevidence; and if [the litigant] wins the case in regard to both the damages for forcible seizure and his rights of ownership, the judge hands him a copy of the court decision with regard to both his rights of ownership and the damages for forcible seizure.

ARTICLE 12. And whoever has won his lawsuit about the ownership of land and the damages for forcible seizure, and has received his copy of the court decision, may proceed to his land, [and if he forcibly ejects his contestant from the land] he is subject to no fine.

ARTICLE 13. And if in any litigation a litigant sues another and that other presents his counterclaims, the matter is brought to the court, and until it is settled neither of the litigants may start any fur-

---

ARTICLE 8. "Sealer," *kliuchnik*. The usual connotation of this Russian term is "home-steward."

ther lawsuits against the other; nor may he instigate Novgorod citizens against his contestant. And he shall swear that he will resort to no subterfuge about it.

ARTICLE 14. Anyone commencing a lawsuit [after the promulgation of this charter] must kiss the cross once, [promising to obey the law]; and if he comes to the court hall without having kissed the cross, he must kiss it and only then is allowed to sue; and if the defendant has not yet kissed the cross after the promulgation of this charter, he likewise must kiss the cross and only then may sue; and if either litigant refuses to kiss the cross he loses his case.

ARTICLE 15. And if a litigant refuses to kiss the cross under the pretext that he is represented by an attorney, he has to kiss the cross once just the same, and only then his attorney may conduct the suit; and if he keeps refusing to kiss the cross, he loses his case.

ARTICLE 16. And if the widow, either of an upper-class man, or of a middle-class burgher, is a defendant in a suit, and she has a son, that son may kiss the cross on behalf of both himself and his mother, once; and if the son refuses to kiss the cross on behalf of his mother, the mother has to kiss the cross in her home in the presence of the plaintiff and of the Novgorod constables.

ARTICLE 17. And in litigations about land the boyar, the middle-class burgher, or the merchant, shall kiss the cross in behalf of himself and his wife.

ARTICLE 18. And if they sue a boyar, or a middle-class burgher, or a merchant for his land or for his wife's land, he may, after having kissed the cross, defend himself, or he may send his attorney in behalf of himself and his wife.

ARTICLE 19. And in litigations about boats the attorney and the witness must kiss the cross.

ARTICLE 20. And the same members of the Court of Reëxamination who accept a case shall conduct it to the conclusion.

ARTICLE 21. And when the assessors state the case, the judge orders his secretary to write down his statement, and the assessors seal the copy.

ARTICLE 22. And it is not permissible to produce a witness against [an already recognized] witness. And neither [an alien, such as] a Pskov citizen, nor a full slave may serve as witness [in regular cases]. But a slave may be a witness against another slave.

ARTICLE 23. And if the litigants refer to a witness, the allowance for travel expenses of the officials [sent for the witness] must be paid in advance: to the sergeant, up to 100 versts, according to old custom; to the constable, or the archbishop's squire, or the herald, or the informer, four *grivna* up to 100 versts. And if a litigant refers to a witness whose residence is more than 100 versts distant, and the other litigant agrees to refer to the same witness, the latter is summoned. But if the other litigant refuses to pay his share for summoning a witness from a distance over 100 versts, he may produce his own witness. And the term for summoning a witness from a distance not over 100 versts is three weeks. And it is the loser of the suit who finally covers the expenses for the summoning of a witness, but the amount is paid in advance to the sergeant.

ARTICLE 24. And if there is a litigation about land, and the defendant asks for a term for obtaining documents or summoning the co-owners of the land [from a distance], the term is three weeks for 100 versts, and proportionally if the distance is more or less than that figure. And he must name his co-owners and indicate specifically where the documents are, supporting his statement by an oath. And he has to strike an agreement with the plaintiff concerning the term, and the mayor has to seal that agreement, and the term may not be changed after that; and the fee for a term agreement is one *grivna*. And [if the case is tried not by the mayor] but by some other judge, he has to confirm the term agreement accordingly. And if a litigant refuses to accept his sealed copy of the term agreement, the judge handling the case shall accuse him without waiting for the expiration of the term. And for other lawsuits the term is appointed according to old customs.

ARTICLE 25. And at the court presided over by the Grand Duke's justice there shall be an assessor for each litigant, and the assessors must be reliable men and must conduct the trial honestly, after being sworn to obey the law according to this charter.

ARTICLE 23. Sergeant, *shestnik;* constable, *podvoisky;* archbishop's squire, *sofian* (literally, "St. Sophia's man," that is, one connected with the Cathedral of St. Sophia) ; herald, *birich.*

ARTICLE 24. Co-owner, *shabr,* in the Charter of the City of Pskov, *siabr,* see that Charter, Article 106, and the corresponding note.

ARTICLE 26. And if the cause has been referred to the superior court [on the judge's recommendation], the Court of Reëxamination meets in the archbishop's hall, with one boyar and one middle-class burgher from each city district present; also present are those judges and assessors who had tried the case in the lower court, as well as the assessors representing the litigants; and no one else is admitted. And the members of the Court of Reëxamination meet thrice a week, on Mondays, Wednesdays, and Fridays. And if a member fails to attend a session, he is fined two rubles, if he is a boyar; and if he is a middle-class burgher, one ruble. And the members of the Court of Reëxamination shall accept no bribes, nor favor any side through some subterfuge, in accordance with their oath. And he who attends the session of the Court of Reëxamination for the first time, must kiss the cross once, [promising to obey the law] according to this charter.

ARTICLE 27. And the mayor, and the chiliarch, and the archbishop's lieutenant, and their judges, and the borough judges all have to kiss the cross [promising] that they will conduct the trials justly.

ARTICLE 28. And the trial of any lawsuit about land has to be completed within two months; and its conclusion may not be delayed over two months. [But if the boundaries have to be examined by a land-surveyor], the mayor has two more months, following the land-surveyor's report, to complete the case, but he may not prolong it over two months. And if the mayor, after having sent the land-surveyor to examine the boundaries, leaves the city [for some private business] without having completed the case, the Grand Dukes and Novgorod the Great fine him 50 rubles, and besides he has to pay the damages to the plaintiff. Likewise, if the chiliarch, or the archbishop's lieutenant, leaves the city before the completion of the case he tries, the Grand Dukes and Novgorod the Great fine him 50 rubles, and besides he has to pay the damages to the plaintiff.

ARTICLE 26. "Court of Reëxamination," *doklad*. In the Novgorod judiciary there was a difference between *peresud* (Court of Appeals) and *doklad* (Court of Reëxamination). In the *peresud* procedure, appeal was made by one of the litigants; the case was reëxamined by the prince's lieutenants and justices; in the *doklad* procedure, the case was referred to the higher court by the judge of the lower court because of the lack of a suitable law or lack of convincing evidence. The case was then reëxamined by a special court, the composition of which is described in this section.

ARTICLE 29. And if a judge has not completed a lawsuit about land within two months, the plaintiff shall receive, for his assistance, sergeants at arms from Novgorod the Great, and the judge shall complete the case in the presence of those sergeants at arms. [And if the judge refers the matter to the Court of Reëxamination] and that Court does not complete the case within two months, the judge [of the lower court] and the plaintiff likewise apply to Novgorod the Great for help and receive sergeants at arms [for compelling] the members of the Court of Reëxamination [to conduct the case without delay]. The Court of Reëxamination shall then instruct the judge [of the lower court] concerning the solution of the case, in the presence of the sergeants at arms, and the judge completes the case in the presence of the said sergeants.

ARTICLE 30. And if any litigants agree upon the time [of the hearing of their case] and each of them receives from the judge a copy of the term agreement, and then the judge is removed, the litigants have to appear before his successor and produce their copies of the term agreement, in time, and that judge shall conduct and complete that case.

ARTICLE 31. And if one of the litigants appears before the judge in time and produces his copy of the term agreement, and the other does not appear [he stands accused, and] the judge issues a writ against him, [a copy of which is handed to that litigant who did appear before the judge]. And to that copy of the writ his copy of the term agreement is attached by seal; and no notice is sent to the defendant.

ARTICLE 32. And if an attorney arranges for a term [of the hearing of the case] in behalf of the claimant and dies before the appointed time, the claimant has either to appear in person before the judge in time, or to send another attorney; and if he fails to appear in person, or to send another attorney, he stands accused.

ARTICLE 33. And if anyone wins a lawsuit about theft on the evidence of the stolen object being found in the home of the defendant, or about robbery, or burglary, or murder, or about a runaway slave, or about a land deed, the judges collect four *grivna* for each court decision, and two *grivna* for each writ.

ARTICLE 34. And if anyone [wins a lawsuit and] receives a copy of the court decision, the defendant must pay his score both to the

---

ARTICLE 29. "Sergeant at arms," *pristav*.

judge [as court fees] and to the plaintiff, within a month. And if he does not settle his score within a month, the plaintiff may apply to the city assembly for constables in order to apprehend the defendant, be it in the city or in a village. And if the defendant hides from the constables, the whole authority of Novgorod the Great is against him.

ARTICLE 35. And if anyone is charged by a witness with some crime, he may challenge the witness within two weeks; and if the witness evades the challenge for two weeks, the defendant approaches the plaintiff; and if the witness hides from the plaintiff, the charges of such a witness are no charges, and the defendant stands acquitted. And if the defendant does not challenge either the witness or the plaintiff within two weeks, [he stands accused], and the judge issues a writ against him on the evidence of the charges.

ARTICLE 36. And if [a Novgorod citizen] charges a man subject to the authority of the archbishop, or of a boyar, or of a middle-class burgher, or of a merchant, or of a monastery, or of a city district guild, or of a street guild, with a crime committed in a country district—such as theft, or robbery, or burglary, or arson, or murder, or with being his runaway slave—the claimant, provided he has been duly sworn to obey the law according to this charter, may present to the authorities his statement, signed by him and confirmed by oath, to the effect that the man he charges is indeed a thief, or a robber, or a burglar, or an incendiary, or a murderer, or [his runaway] slave. And the archbishop's officials in the country district [referred to by the claimant]—the bailiff, or the village steward—must bring that [suspected] man to the court; and the boyar, or the middle-class burgher, or the merchant, or the monastery bailiff or the village steward, or the city district elder, or the street elder, likewise must bring that [suspected] man to the court. And the term [for producing him] is three weeks for a distance of 100 versts, and more or less proportionally. And nobody shall abuse him prior to the hearing of the case in the court; and whoever abuses him, himself stands accused.

ARTICLE 36. "Street," *ulitsa*. In Novgorod the inhabitants of each "city district" (*konets*) and of each "street" formed a self-governing association, or guild, each under an elected "elder" (*starosta*). Bailiff, *volostel*.

ARTICLE 37. And if a man charged [with a crime or claimed by the plaintiff as his runaway slave] registers as the slave of another, the [new] owner may not keep him in his house; and if he keeps him and is detected, he has to pay damages. Nor may the owner send that man away into another country district; if sent away, the man has to be surrendered to the plaintiff. And no country district authorities shall accept that man, in accordance with their oath. [All the above regulations are issued for the cases of this nature only] and in other kinds of cases the litigants deal with each other [without the assistance of the said authorities]. And if anyone kisses the cross and signs the promise that he will not keep that [suspected] man in his country district, [and keeps him] and is detected, he has to pay the damages to the plaintiff. And if the man moves into another country district, its authorities must bring him to the court, according to their oath; and if they fail to bring him to the court, they are fined in accordance with the Novgorod Charter.

ARTICLE 38. And if anyone charges a man subject to the authority of the archbishop or of a boyar, or of a middle-class burgher, or of a merchant, or of a monastery, or of a city district guild, or of a street guild, with some crime, and has not kissed the cross to obey the law according to this charter, he has to deal directly with the defendant.

ARTICLE 39. And whoever has agreed upon the time of his appearing before the court, no notices are sent to him; but if the judge postpones the term, he shall send notices to the litigants. And if a litigant hides from being served the notice, the notice is sent to him thrice, and he is called by a herald; if he does not then appear before the court, a writ is issued against him for the breach of a pledge and he is fined to an amount not over 3 *denga*.

ARTICLE 40. And if [the defendant's partisans] seize the plaintiff in a village and abuse him, his nearest relative or friend receives from the judge a writ in his behalf against the defendant.

ARTICLE 41. And when a claimant summons the other claimant from a village through a messenger or a squire, the term is two weeks for 100 versts, and more or less proportionally.

ARTICLE 37. The text of this clause is obscure and contains repetitions. Its object apparently is to prevent a suspected criminal from evading justice by giving himself into slavery.

ARTICLE 42. Two men shall represent [in the court] a city district, or a street, or a hundred, or a row [in the litigations involving inhabitants of any of the town communities]; and no other men are to be let in to the court hall or allowed to take part in the hearing. And if [besides those two appointed men] the defendant's partisans from a city district, or street, or hundred, or row, throng in the court hall, the Grand Dukes and Novgorod the Great, in accordance with this charter, [fine] those two men. . . .

GLOSSARY

BELA, silver coin; fur, presumably ermine.
BIRICH, herald, public announcer.
BLOODWITE, *vira*, a fine payable to the prince for the murder.
BOT, *golovnichestvo*, amends payable to the relatives of the murdered man.
BRATCHINA, a banquet fraternity. (See notes to Articles 34 and 113, pp. 68, 81.)
CHELIADIN, a member of the lord's household; a slave.
CHERNYE LIUDI, literally "black men," men of lower classes.
DACHA, grant. (See note, Article 111, pp. 54, 55.)
DENGA, a term borrowed from the Mongolian: a monetary unit. In modern Russian the plural form *dengi*, is still used to denote "money."
DIKAIA VIRA, "dark" bloodwite, that is, bloodwite paid by the members of the guild collectively, especially when the murderer is unknown. (See notes to Articles 3–8, pp. 36, 37.)
DOKLAD, in Novgorod, Court of Reëxamination; proceedings by which a case was referred to the higher court by the judge of the lower court.
DOSKA, tally, writing tablet; a noncertified note.
DVORIANIN, a princely servitor of lower grade; in modern Russian, a nobleman.

GOLOVA, head, *see* WERGELD.
GOLOVNICHESTVO, see BOT.
GOSPODA, in Pskov, the Supreme Court; in Novgorod, the House of Lords.
GRIVNA, monetary unit. (See Introduction, Section VII, p. 24.)
GUILD, see VERV'.
IABETNIK, agent; in Norwegian laws, *umbodsmadr*.
ISAD, a fishery establishment.
IZGOI, in the twelfth century, a freedman. However, as used in the Short Version of the Russian Law, the term must have had a different connotation. (See note to Article 1, pp. 26, 27.)
IZORNIK, tenant farmer.
KHOLOP, slave.
K'HOP, presumably, a herdsman of Patzinak extraction. (See note to Article 26, p. 32.)
KLIUCHNIK, a home steward; in Novgorodian administration, sealer.
KNIAZH MUZH, literally, the prince's man; a princely official, a boyar.
KOCHETNIK, fisherman.
KOLBIAG. (See note to Article 10, pp. 27, 28.)
KONETS, in Novgorod, a city district.
KONIUKH STARY, steward of grooms; master of stables.
KOSTKI, a tax on merchandise.
KUNA, marten fur; a monetary unit. (See Introduction, Section VII, p. 24.)

GLOSSARY

LIUDIN, a man; a member of the guild; a commoner.
LIUDSKAIA VIRA, literally "men's bloodwite"; bloodwite paid by the members of the guild collectively (see DIKAIA VIRA).

MECHNIK, sheriff. (See note to Article 1, p. 26.)
METALNIK, METELNIK, sheriff.
MIR, community; township.
MOLODCHI CHELOVEK, literally "younger man," a lower-class burgher.
MUZH, a man; a man of noble birth, a knight.
MYT, custom duties.

NAMESTNIK, lieutenant.
NOGATA, monetary unit. (See Introduction, Section VII, p. 24.)

OGNISHCHANIN, a man belonging to the prince's hearth; princely servitor; bailiff.
OGNISHCHE, hearth.
OGORODNIK, gardener, vegetable gardener.

PERESUD, in Novgorod, Court of Appeals; appeals procedure.
PIR, banquet. See BRATCHINA.
PODIEZDNOI, messenger, adjutant.
PODVOISKY, constable.
POKRUTA, in Pskov, subsidy in money or seeds granted by the owner of the land to the tenant farmer.
POLE, literally, field; duel field, hence, judicial duel.
POSADNIK, mayor.
POSLUKH, witness. (See Introduction, Section II, p. 11.)
PRIGOROD, borough, literally "by-town."
PRISTAV, constable.

PRODAZHA, a fine payable to the prince.

REZANA, monetary unit. (See Introduction, Section VII, p. 24.)
RIADOVICH, contract laborer.
ROLIA, plow land.
ROTÁ, oath as part of the court procedure.

SAMOSUD, taking the law in one's own hands; settling with the criminal in a private way. (See Article 6 of the Charter of Dvina Land, p. 58, and the corresponding note.)
SHABR, a co-owner; a member of a coöperative corporation.
SHESTNIK, infantry soldier; a sergeant.
SIABR, variant of shabr.
SKOTNIK, in Pskov, a dealer in cattle. (See note to Article 18, p. 65.)
SLUGA, literally, servitor; in late Middle Ages, a princely councilor of second class, lower than a boyar.
SMERD, peasant. (See note to Article 26, pp. 32. 33.)
SOBOR, cathedral; in Pskov, also an ecclesiastical district.
SOFIAN, literally, St. Sophia's man, that is, one connected with the cathedral of St. Sophia in Novgorod; a squire in the service of the Archbishop of Novgorod.
SOTNIK, hundreder.
STAROSTA, elder, alderman.
SVOD, "confrontation," examination; procedure for identifying a thief. (See note to Article 14, and Introduction, Section II, pp. 11, 28.)

TAMGA, a term borrowed from the Mongolian: internal customs duty.

GLOSSARY

TAT', a thief; a robber.
TIUN, a steward; a justice.
TIUN KONIUSHII, master of stables.
TIUN OGNISHCHNY, bailiff. (See OGNISHCHANIN.)
TIVUN, variant of TIUN.
TIVUNETS, assistant steward.
TYSIATSKY, chiliarch; commander of the "thousand," that is, of the city militia. In Novgorod court system, the chiliarch was in charge of the conduct of litigations about commercial transactions.

ULITSA, street; in Novgorod, an association of neighbors living in the same street, a guild.

VDACH, the recipient of a grant (*dacha*). (See note to Article 111, pp. 54, 55.)
VECHE, people's assembly; city assembly.
VEKSHA, literally, a squirrel; a monetary unit. (See Introduction, Section VII, p. 24.)
VERST, VERSTA, measure of length, equal to 0.6 miles.
VERV', guild; an association of neighbors in a country district.
VEVERITSA, see VEKSHA.
VIDOK, eyewitness.
VIRA, see BLOODWITE.
VIRNIK, collector of bloodwite payments.
VOLOST', a country district.
VOLOSTEL, bailiff.

WERGELD: GOLOVA, ZA GOLOVU, literally, "head"; the value of the head, that is, the value set on a man's life. It is according to that value that the normal amount of the bot as well as that of the bloodwite was computed.

ZAKUP, indentured laborer. (See note to Article 56, p. 46.) *Roleinyi Zakup*, agricultural laborer; see ROLIA.
ZAKUPEN, in Pskov, a purchasing agent. (See note to Article 18, p. 65.)
ZHIT'I LIUDI, in Novgorod, middle-class burghers.

BIBLIOGRAPHY

GENERAL

Diakonov, M. A., Ocherki obshchestvennogo i gosudarstvennogo stroia Drevnei Rusi (4th ed., St. Petersburg, 1912).
Dovnar-Zapolsky, M. V., Istoriia Russkogo narodnogo khoziaistva, Vol. I (Kiev, 1911).
Eck, A., Le Moyen Âge russe (Brussels, 1933).
Grushevsky, M. S. (Hrushevsky, M.), Istoriia Ukrainy-Rusi, Vols. I–IV (Lviv, 1903–1905).
Kliuchevsky, V. O., A History of Russia, trans. by Hogarth, Vols. I–II (New York, 1911–1912).
Larson, L. M., The Earliest Norwegian Laws (New York, 1935).
Presniakov, A. E., Lektsii po russkoi istorii, Vols. I–II (Moscow, 1938).
Saturník, T., Přispěvky k šiření Byzantského práva u Slovanů (Prague, 1922).
Vernadsky, G., Political and Diplomatic History of Russia (Boston, 1936).
Vladimirsky-Budanov, V. F., Khristomatiia po istorii russkogo prava, Vol. I (6th ed., St. Petersburg and Kiev, 1908).
——— Obzor istorii russkogo prava (7th ed., Petrograd and Kiev, 1915).

NUMISMATICS

Il'in, A. A., Klassifikatsiia russkikh udelnykh monet, Vol. I (Leningrad, 1940).
Kaufman, I., Serbrianyi rubl' v Rossii (St. Petersburg, 1910).
Markov, A., Russkaia numizmatika (Petrograd, 1915).
Prozorovsky, D. I., Moneta i ves v Rossii (St. Petersburg, 1865).
Tolstoy, Count I. I., "Drevneishie russkie monety," *Zapiski* of the Russian Archeological Society, VI (1893), 310–382.

THE RUSSIAN LAW

Editions and Translations

Goetz, L. K., Das russische Recht, Vol. I (Stuttgart, 1910), pp. 6–65. A reproduction of Sergeevich's edition, with a German translation.
Grekov, B. D., ed., Pravda Russkaia, Vol. I (Moscow-Leningrad, 1940).
Iushkov, S. V., ed., Rus'ka Pravda (Kiev, 1935).
Sergeevich, V. I., Russkaia Pravda (St. Petersburg, 1904).
Wiener, L., Anthology of Russian Literature, Vol. I (New York and London,

1902), pp. 45–48. A partial English translation inadequate from the point of view of legal history.

Studies

Efron, A. B., Etiudy po istorii russkogo iuridicheskogo byta, Vol. I (Brussels, 1939).
Goetz, L. K., Das russische Recht (Stuttgart, 1910–1915), Vols. I–IV.
Grekov, B. D., Kievskaia Rus' (4th ed., Moscow-Leningrad, 1944).
Iushkov, S. V., Narysy z istorii vynyknennia i pochatkovogo rozvytku feodalizmu v Kyivskii Rusi (Kiev, 1939).
Mrochek-Drozdovsky, P., "Opyt izsledovaniia istochnikov po voprosu o dengakh Russkoi Pravdy," *Uchenye Zapiski* of the Moscow University, Juridical Section, Vol. II (Moscow, 1881).
―――― "Izsledovaniia o Russkoi Pravde," *Ibid.*, Vol. IV (Moscow, 1885).
Obnorsky, S. P., "Russkaia Pravda kak pamiatnik russkogo literaturnogo iazyka," *Izvestiia Akademii Nauk*, Series VII (1934), pp. 749–776.
Tikhomirov, M. N., Issledovaniie o Russkoi Pravde, Vol. I (Moscow-Leningrad, 1941).
Vernadsky, G., "Three Notes on the Social History of Kievan Russia," *Slavonic and East European Review*, XXII (1944), 81–92.

The Charter of Dvina Land

Tobien, E. S., Die aelteste Gerichtsordnungen Russlands (Dorpat, 1846), pp. 32–36.
Vladimirsky-Budanov, Khristomatiia, Vol. I (St. Petersburg and Kiev, 1908), pp. 121–127.

The Charter of the City of Pskov

Editions

Cherepnin, L. V., and A. I. Iakovlev, "Pskovskaia sudnaia gramota," *Istoricheskie Zapiski*, 1940, No. 6, pp. 237–299. This is a translation into modern Russian.
Miklosich, F., and I. Fiedler, eds., Slawische Bibliothek, Vol. II (Vienna, 1858).
Pskovskaia sudnaia Gramota, ed. by the Archaeographic Commission (St. Petersburg, 1914). A phototypic reproduction of the manuscript.
Vladimirsky-Budanov, V. F., Khristomatiia, Vol. I (St. Petersburg & Kiev, 1908), pp. 128–162.

Studies

Argunov, P. A., "Krestianin i zemlevladelets v epokhu Pskovskoi Sudnoi Gramoty," *Uchenye Zapiski* of Saratov University, Vol. IV (1925).
Bogoslovsky, M. M., "K voprosu ob otnosheniiakh krestianina k zemlevladeltsu po Pskovskoi Sudnoi Gramote," *Letopis Zaniatii* of the Archaeographic Commission, XXXIV (1927), 27–54.

Engelman, I., Sistematicheskoe izlozhenie grazhdanskikh zakonov, soderzhashchikhsia v Pskovskoi Sudnoi Gramote (St. Petersburg, 1855).

Grekov, B. D., "Zemledelets i zemlevladelets v Pskove XV v.," *Problemy Istorii Dokapitalisticheskikh Obshchestv*, 1934, No. 5, pp. 54–82.

Mikhailov, P. E., Iuridicheskaia priroda zemlepolzovaniia po Pskovskoi Sudnoi Gramote (St. Petersburg, 1914). (Inaccessible to me.)

Nikitsky, A., Ocherk vnutrennei istorii Pskova (St. Petersburg, 1873).

Pushkarev, S. G., "Vnitřní zřizení a vnějši postavení Pskovského státu," *Sborník věd právnich a státnich*, XXV (1925).

Rozhkova, M. K., K voprosu o proiskhozhdenii i sostave Pskovskoi Sudnoi Gramoty (Leningrad-Moscow, 1927). (Inaccessible to me.)

Ustrialov, F., Izsledovanie Pskovskoi Sudnoi Gramoty (St. Petersburg, 1855).

THE CHARTER OF THE CITY OF NOVGOROD

Kostomarov, N. I., Severno-russkiia narodopravstva, Vol. II (St. Petersburg, 1863). A study on the history of Novgorod.

Nikitsky, A., "Istoriia ekonomicheskogo byta Velikogo Novgoroda," *Chteniia* of the Society of Russian History and Antiquities, 1893, I–II.

―――― Ocherk vnutrennei istorii tserkvi v Velikom Novgorode (St. Petersburg, 1879).

―――― "Ocherki iz zhizni Velikogo Novgoroda," I–II, *Zhurnal Ministerstva Narodnogo Prosveshcheniia*, CXLV (1869), 294–309; CL (1870), 201–224.

Vladimirsky-Budanov, V. F., Khristomatiia, I (St. Petersburg and Kiev, 1908), pp. 172–185. An edition of the Charter.

INDEX

Academy copy of Short Version, 13 (see also under Law, Russian: Short Version
Academy of Sciences, Russian, 13
Academy of Sciences, Ukrainian, 14
Academy of Sciences of the U.S.S.R., Historical Institute, 14
Alexander, Grand Duke, charter, 61
Alexander Nevsky, Grand Duke, 17
Alexander of Tver, Grand Duke, 61n
Alfred, king, Wessex laws, 4
Animals, domestic: litigations about, 28, 32, 41, 42, 47, 50, 81
Apiary, cutting boundary of, 49; litigation about, 80
Apprentice, master sues, 79
Archaeographic Commission copy of Short Version, 13
Archbishop's court, 62, 81, 83
Arm cut off, 27, 39
Arson, 82
Assessors, 84, 87
Attorney, 74; dies before term of hearing, 89; not allowed in court, 73

Bailiff, murder of, 30, 31; peasant inflicts pain on, 49
Baltic, German expansion in the, 6
Beard, injury to, 27, 48, 82
Beating, 39, 65; of indentured laborer, 47
Beehive, damage to, 33, 48, 49
Beloozero Charter of 1488, 7
Bequests, see Inheritance
Bishop's court, see Church courts
Blood revenge, 26, 35; custom canceled, 35
Bloodwite, distribution of payments, 33, 34; guild has to pay a "dark," 36; if defendant rejects, 38; in case of a reported homicide, 38
Bloodwite collector, pay and provisions, 34, 37, 49
Boat, stealing, 33, 49
Boundaries, contested, 76; plowing beyond, 33, 49, 58
Boyar, estate of, 51; offense to, 58
Branding of thieves, 12
Bribery, 58, 59, 62

Bridgebuilders, payments, 34, 52
Bruises, smeared with blood, or blue from, 32, 39
Byzantium, money economy, 9

Capital punishment, 12, 63n
Capitularia of the Frankish kings, 5
Carpenter may sue employer, 69
Cattle, killing, 32; stealing, 41, 42; indentured laborer's liability for, 47; injury to, 50; see also Cow
Charters, 7, 13, 57–92; see also under Dvina Land; Novgorod; Pskov
Cherepnin, L. V., and A. I. Iakovlev, 75n
Chiliarch of Novgorod, 83n, 84
Christianity, Russia officially converted to, 34n
Chudin, princely councilor, 30
Chudinovich, Ivanko, see Ivanko Chudinovich
Church, a factor in development of law and legislation, 3, 9; in political life of Novgorod, 18; passage in Pravda shows influence of, 34n
Church courts, 10, 62, 81, 83
Church land, litigations about, 74
Church Statute of Vladimir the Saint, 5
Codes, see Law, Russian
Collector of fines, see Bloodwite collector
Commercial loans, 79
Commercial treaties, Russian-German, 6
Community, see Social unit
Confrontment, 11, 29, 40, 41
Constables, tax to, from boat, 59; allowance for travel expenses, 71, 74; and prince's men shall travel in pairs, 71, 76; investigation of theft, 72
Constantine, prince, charter, 61
Constantine Porphyrogenitus, emperor, 32n
Contract laborer, murder of, 32, 38
Cook, killing, 37
Coöperative corporation, litigation re share in, 78, 80
Corporal punishment, 12
Court, assistants to litigants not allowed in,

INDEX

Court (*Continued*)
73; cause referred to superior court, 88; failure to appear in, 59; fees, 53, 85, 89, 90; litigants only, allowed in court, 73; postponement of term, 91; representatives in, of city district, or street, 92; trial, *see* Lawsuit
Court decision, copy of, 59
"Court Law for the People," 6
Court of Appeals, 84*n*, 88*n*
Court of Reëxamination, 86, 88, 89
Courts, church, 10, 62, 81, 83
Courts of the prince, coöperation with institutions of the people, 9 f.
Cow, gives birth to calf, 82; killing, 32
Craftsman, *see* Handicraftsman
Crime, committed in country district, 90; composition of, by money, 35
Criminal, gives himself into slavery, 91; settling privately with, *see* Bribery
Cross, *see* Kissing the cross
Currency, *see* Money
Customary law, Russian, 14

Damage, paying for, 29
Deathbed gifts, 79
Debtor fails to appear in court, 78
Debts, 46; of father divided among sons, 78; who may hire substitute fighter for duel, 68; *see also* Loans
Deeds as proof at court trial, 12
Diakonov, M. A., 75*n*
Documents, as proof at court trial, 12; stealing, 59; translation, 21
Dovnar-Zapolsky, M. V., 44*n*
Drunkenness, exchange or sale while in state of, 81
Duel, 11, 12; between women, 82; litigation decided by, 69; right to hire a substitute, 66
Dvina Land, 20 f.; Charter of, 7, 13, 21, 57-60; grand-ducal constables shall not enter, 59

Ecclesiastical courts, *see* Church courts
Ecloga, 5
Economic life, evidence on, found in legal clauses, 8
Efron, A. B., 32*n*
Engelman, I. E., 62*n*
Estates, disposal of, *see* Inheritance
Extortion, 71
Eye, injury to, 39

Farmer, subsidy from landlord, 71; *see also* Tenant farmer

Farm manager, murder of, 31
Field overseer, murder of, 31
Fight, at a banquet, 58; between a number of men, 82; in public place, 67; settled by apologies, 76
Fines, *see* Bloodwite, payments
Fingers, injury to, 27, 39
Fishery, establishment fraudulently obtained, 74 f.; lessee misses spring catch, 70
Foreigner sues native, 80
Fraternity, judicial authority, 81
Furs as currency, 23 f.

Game, theft of, 48
God, appeal to judgment of, 11; habitual approach to, in court procedure, 11
Goetz, L. K., 14, 31, 44*n*
Greek Orthodox Church forbade practice of usury, 8
Grekov, B. D., 26*n*, 35*n*, 46
Grivna, 24; relation of *kuna* to, 45*n*
Groom, killing, 37
Guarantee, 79
Guild, collective responsibility of members, 36; murder within boundaries of, 31, 36; must search for poacher, 48; *see also* Social unit

Handicraftsman, may sue employer, 69; penalty for killing, 38; protected by legislation, 15
Hay, stealing, 50
Herdsman, murder of, 32
Historical Institute of the Academy of Sciences, 14
Hitting, *see* Striking
Homestead, given to youngest son, 52; suit for, 84
Homicide, 36; bloodwite, 38
Horse, injury to, 50; killing prince's or peasant's, 32; riding another's, 28; stealing, 32, 42, 47
Hundreder, tax to, from boat, 59
Hunting nets, 50

Iakovlev, A. I., L. V. Cherepnin and, 75*n*
Iaroslav the Wise, 29*n*; first code of laws compiled in reign of, 4; his *Pravda* connected with Novgorod charters, 14; Ordinances of Iaroslav son of Vladimir, 35 ff.; *see also* Law, Russian: Short Version
Incendiary, 63
Indentured laborer, 46, 47; cannot serve as witness, 48

INDEX

Inheritance, 51, 52, 53, 64; if son leaves home, 72; law, 16; several claimants, 80
Injuries, personal, 27, 39, 48, 57
Interest, see Loans
Intimidation, 84
Iron, ordeal by, 38, 50
Istoriia Gosudarstva Rossiikogo (Karamzin), 20
Iushkov, S. V., 14
Ivan III, grand duke, 19, 63n, 83
Ivan Ivanovich, grand duke, 83
Ivanko Chudinovich, princely councilor, 44
Izgoi, term, 23, 26n
Iziaslav, Prince of Kiev, 15, 29, 35

Judge, fees, 89; removed before completion of trial, 89

Karamzin, N. M., 20, 21
Kazimir IV, king of Poland, 19
Kiev, authority of princes of Riurik dynasty, 3; riots, 16; rivalry between Novgorod and, 17
Kievan Russia, economic growth: agriculture and commerce, 9; social gulf between propertied classes and labor, 8
Kissing the cross, 11 f., 86
Kliuchevsky, V. O., 44n, 45n
Knight, offense to, 58
Kolbiag, exempt from normal court procedure, 27
Kosniachko, princely councilor, 30, 35
Kremlin thief, 63n
Kuna, 24; relation to *grivna*, 45n

Laborer, hired, may sue for wages, 69; indentured, 46, 47, 48; murder of contract laborer, 32, 38
Land, forcible seizure and robbery, 85; fraudulently obtained, 74 f.; lawsuit about ownership, 85; litigations about church land, 74; litigation between owner and group of coöperative owners, 80; litigation concerning cultivated, 63; plaintiff may not seize, in suit for homestead, 84; term agreement in litigation, 87; term for trial, 88, 89; who shall read deed, 76
Landlord, lodger may sue, 79
Law, Byzantine: ties between Russian law and, 5
Law, Frankish, 4
Law, German: capital punishment the result of influence of, 12; evolution of medieval Russian laws similar to that of, 3, 6; norms borrowed in laws of Novgorod and Pskov, 6
Law, Muscovite, 7
Law, Russian: three main factors, 3, 9; Code of 1497, 7
——— *Pravda Russkaia*, 4, 12 ff., 26-56
——— Short Version, 5, 7, 13, 26-35; Academy copy, 13; Grekov's edition, 26n; Archaeographic Commission copy, 13; *Iaroslav's Pravda*: 4, 13, 14, 26-29; two basic copies, 13; *Pravda of Iaroslav's sons*: 4 ff., 10, 14, 29-35
——— Expanded Version, 5, 7, 8, 10, 13, 35-56; manuscript copies, 13; three parts, 15; Trinity copy, 13; Grekov's edition, 35n; *revised Pravda of Iaroslav's sons*: 15, 16, 35-43; *Abridged Version*: 13; *Statute of Vladimir Monomach*: 8, 15, 16, 43-48
Laws, Wessex, 4
Lawsuit, authority of Grand Duke's justices to reëxamine causes in appeal proceedings, 84; case written and sealed, 86; concerning new trial, 73; fee for loss of, 59; modes of proof at trial, 11 f.; must be conducted justly, 76, 88; if litigant refuses to accept term agreement, 87; term of conduct of trial, 85; trials by archbishop's lieutenants, prince, or mayor, 62; when litigants come to agreement, 74
Lease, termination of, 70; termination of tenant farmer's, 74
Leg cut off, 27, 39
Legal history, trends, 3
Lex Russica, see Law, Russian: *Pravda Russkaia*
Lex Salica, 4
Lithuanian Statute, 13
Litigant, accused, does not appear before judge, 89; claims and counterclaims, 85
Loans, attitude of *Pravda* and city charters toward usury, 8; commercial, 79; interest, 8, 9, 43, 44, 45, 75; litigation concerning, 67, 69, 70; reclaiming pledge on, 80; suing for, 42
Lodger may sue landlord, 79
"Lord Pskov," 20

Magdeburg law, 6
Master of the stable, murder of, 31
Mayor, may not serve as attorney for another, 74; of Novgorod, 83n; trials by, 62
Mechnik, term, 26n

INDEX

Merchants, laws governing, 60; liability in case of shipwreck, 45
"Metropolitan's Justice," 5
Mikula, princely councilor, 30, 34n
Mikyfor (or Nikifor), the Kievan, princely councilor, 30
Miroslav, princely councilor, 44
Miscarriage, 79
Monetary units, 23
Money, furs as currency, 23 f.; suing for, 42; see also Loans
Moscow, Grand Duke of, control in central Russia, 7
Moscow, ascendancy, 7
Mrochek-Drozdovsky, P. N., 24
Municipal law, German, 6
Murder, avengers, 26, 35; of master of prince's stables, 15; penalties for, 30 ff., 51, 57, 66; prince collects fine, 79; while stealing, 31, 33; without provocation, 36
Murzakevich, N. N., 20
Mustache, loss of, 27
Muzh, term, 26n

Nazhir, princely councilor, 44
Nevsky, Alexander, see Alexander Nevsky
Nikifor, see Mikyfor
Nose, injury to, 39
Note, litigation on basis of a certified, 79
Novgorod, 17 ff.; Charter of the City of, 7, 8, 12 f., 17, 83-92; charters granted by Iaroslav, 14; combination of courts: division of competence in judicial matters, 10; rivalry between Kiev and, 17

Oath, 11, 27n; defendant fails to appear to take, 79; fees for administering, 54, 59
Officials, prince's: estates, 51; killing, 37 f.; shall travel in pairs, 71, 76
—— public: allowance for travel expenses, 71, 87; may not serve as attorney for another, 74
Oleg, prince, 44n, 45
Ordeals, 12; by iron, 38, 50; by water, 38
Ox, killing, 32

Page, killing, 37
Partnership, withholding share in, 29
Passport, 77
Peasant, estate of deceased, 51; inflicting pain on, without prince's order, 33, 49; murder of, 32, 48
Penal law, 12
Pereneg, princely councilor, 30, 35
Personal injuries, punishment for inflicting, 27, 39, 48, 57

Pledge, as evidence of obligation, 79; breach of, 91; certificates, 67
Plowing beyond bound or hedge, 33, 49, 58
Poaching, 48
Porphyrogenitus, Constantine, see Constantine Porphyrogenitus
Porters at trial, 73
Poslukh, 11; see also under Witnesses
Poultry, 81
Pravda, term, 3
Pravda Russkaia, see Law, Russian: *Pravda Russkaia*
Pravosudie Mitropolichie, 5
Prince a factor in development of law and legislation, 3, 9
Princely court, 62
Prince's officials or retinue, see Officials, prince's
Prochiron, 5
Prokopii, chiliarch, 44
Property appropriated by brother or nephew, 79; bequest challenged, 72; claim against executor, 64; damage to, 29; deathbed gifts, 79; homestead given to youngest son, 52; suit for homestead, 84; see also Inheritance; Land
Prozorovsky, D. I., 24
Pskov, Lord, charter alteration referred to, 81
Pskov, 19 f.; Charter of the City of, 7, 8, 12 f., 17, 19, 61-82; combination of courts, 10
Pskov Kremlin, Holy Trinity Cathedral, 61
Pulling or pushing, 27, 39
Punishment, capital, 12, 63n; transition from blood revenge to, 12

Ratibor, chiliarch, 44
Rioting in court hall, 12
Robber, see Thief
Robbery, see Stealing
Rostislav, Prince of Smolensk and of Kiev, 17
Rotá, 11; see also Oath
Russische Recht, Das (Goetz), 14
Russo-Byzantine treaty of 945, 14
Russo-German commercial treaties, 6
Russo-German struggle, 18

Sachsenspiegel, 6
Schloezer, A. L., 13
Schub, 11
Scribe, prince's: fee, 71, 76, 77
Security for loan, 67
Sergeevich, V. I., 14
Shackling, fee for, 58

INDEX

Sheep, killing, 32
Shipwreck, liability of merchant in case of, 45
Shuisky, F. Iu., prince, 61
Slave, abducting another's, 32; aiding or concealing, 28, 55; as witness, 48, 50, 86; criminal registers as, to evade justice, 91; inheritance of children by a female slave, 52; killing, 51, 59; murder of slave tutor or nurse, 32; re-claiming runaway, 29, 41; runaway indentured laborer becomes, 46; strikes a freeman, 29, 47; who are thieves, 42, 47, 56
Slavery, 54 ff.; if lord sells indentured labor into, 47; juridical nature of, 16
Smolensk, monetary system, 24; treaty with German cities, 17
Social life, evidence on, found in legal clauses, 8
Social unit, assistance to plaintiff, 10; a factor in development of law and legislation, 3, 9; see also Guild
Spy, 63
Stanislav, chiliarch, 44
Statute of Vladimir Monomach, 8, 15, 16, 43-48
Stealing, 28, 33, 40, 62, 65, 68, 74; in Pskov Kremlin, 63; prince's fine, 72
Stepfather, 52, 53
Steward, murder of prince's, 31
Stocks for rioters, 12
Stolen goods, bought in foreign land, 71; bought at market, 72; buying, 40; found in another's house, 70; holder of, 58; suing seller, 72
Storage, 43, 65
Striking, in court hall, 81; with unsheathed sword, 27; with weapon or fist, 27, 39
Summons, disregard of, 66; fee for serving, 59
Superior court, 88
Sviatoslav, prince, 29, 35
Svod, see Confrontment
Sword, unsheathing, 27; wounding or killing with, 39
Synodal copy of Expanded Version, 13

Tatishchev, V. N., 13
Taverns, prince's men may not keep, 82
Taxation, excessive, 59
Team, 11
Teeth, injury to, 48
Tenant farmer, leaves farm illegally, 75; rights of landlord and descendants of deceased, 77; subsidy from landlord, 71; sues landlord, 75, 77; termination of lease, 74
Term-writ, 10
Theft, see Stealing
Theophilus, Hieromonk, 83
Thief, branding of, 12; deposition to be examined, 73; hung for third offense, 58; killing of, 33; slave who is a, 42
Thief-murderer, 31
Threshing court, 50
Tikhomirov, M. N., 13
Toll on boatload or wagonload, 60
Town walls, payments to builder, 52
Translation of documents, 21
Trial, see Lawsuit
Tribe, see Social unit
Trinity copy of Expanded Version, 13 (see also under Law, Russian: Expanded Version)
Troitsky spisok, Trinity copy of Expanded Version, 13

Ukrainian Academy of Sciences, 14
Ustrialov, F. N., 75n
Usury, see Loans, interest

Varangian, exempt from normal court procedure, 27
Vasili I, Grand Duke of Moscow, 57; charter, 21; see also Dvina Land, Charter of
Vasili II, Grand Duke of Moscow, 19, 61n
Vasili Dmitrievich, see Vasili I
Vasilievich, Ivan, grand duke, see Ivan III
Vasmer, Max, 28n
Vidok, 11, 27n; see also under Witnesses
Vladimir the Saint, Church Statute of, 5
Vladimir Monomach, Prince of Kiev, 14, 16; Statute of, 8, 15, 16, 43-48
Vladimirsky-Budanov, M. F., 34n, 57n, 61n, 83n
Vorontsov, M. S., count, 20
Vsevolod, prince, 29, 35

Wanstrat, Louise, 26n
Water, litigation concerning, 63; ordeal by, 38; who shall read deed to, 76
Weichbild, 6
Widow, does not inherit estate, 51; right to her jewels or clothes, 78; use of husband's property, 77; who agrees to manage estate, 53
Wife, property of deceased, 77, 78; see also Widow
Wills, 51
Witness, 11, 50, 66, 86; evades challenge, 90; eyewitness, 11, 27n; slave or inden-

Witness (*Continued*)
   tured laborer cannot serve as, 48; term for summoning, 87

Women, inheritance, 51, 52, 53; killing, 38, 51; protection of handicrafts women, 15; *see also* Widow; Wife

Woodland, litigation concerning, 63

Worker, hired: may sue for wages, 69

Writ against claimant, 66

Zakon, term, 3

Zakon Russkii, 14

Zakon Sudnyi Liudem, 5 f.

Zweikampf, 12